A TEENAGER'S GUIDE ~~...ING THEIR TRUE CALLING~~ ...LING

THROAT PUNCH NORMAL

JOE ELLIOTT

WITH ZAC TINNEY

THROAT PUNCH NORMAL

A TEENAGER'S GUIDE TO FINDING THEIR TRUE CALLING

JOE ELLIOTT
WITH ZAC TINNEY

MASTER DESIGN PUBLISHING

FULTON, KENTUCKY

Master Design Publishing
  an imprint of Master Design Marketing, LLC
789 State Route 94 E
Fulton, KY 42041
www.MasterDesign.org

Additional chapters by Zac Tinney
Book Layout by Faithe Thomas
Illustrated by Jeff Macpherson at www.JeffryMacpherson.com

Throat Punch Normal/ Joe Elliott. -- 1st ed.
Paperback ISBN 978-1-941512-27-2
Ebook ISBN 978-1-941512-28-9
Hardback ISBN 978-1-941512-29-6

CONTENTS

SECTION 4 YOUR STRATEGY

SECTION 5 YOUR ENEMY

SECTION 6 YOUR PERSPECTIVE

ACKNOWLEDGEMENTS

This book would not be possible without the faithful support and encouragement we have received by so many over the years. We would like to thank our amazing team of editors: Vivian Cullipher, Lyndsie Beesley and Faith Elliott for making this book even better. Thank you to our Board of Directors whose commitment to our mission and vision at The Catalyst Collective has been such an answer to prayer. And finally, to all of our volunteers, donors, and family members who have poured in their time, talent and resources to bring this organization to life – we are deeply grateful. Together we are able to do something far greater than we could ever do alone – and we are only just getting started.

INTRODUCTION

M uch of my hesitation in going all in with Jesus came from the fact that I just didn't feel like I had much to offer. I had felt average my entire life. I did a lot of stuff but I never really excelled at anything. I didn't know what my passions were or even what made me unique. I became content sitting on the bench watching other Christians in action. This book not only chronicles the pathway I went on in going from your 'average Joe' to discovering and owning my God-given gifts and passions, but it is also a collection of some of the most impacting tools and exercises we have ever seen students, like yourself, respond to.

My co-author, and partner in crime, Zac Tinney, has done a brilliant job in offering his insight and wisdom throughout this book. As a Millennial himself, Zac is on the frontlines shaping some of our most innovative programs and content at Catalyst. Having found and embraced his own unique identity through building this ministry with me, Zac can also attest to the power of these exercises.

We wrote this book together because we feel that your generation has the potential to model Jesus to the world better than any other generation in the last century. Reading books may not be your thing but we hope that living a life that truly impacts others is. Put in the work to go through each chapter and we promise it will radically open your eyes to how God has intentionally shaped you and why it matters.

A little something about me (Joe) that you might relate to

The first thing I do when I pick up a book from an author I have never heard of is to flip to the back, because I am interested in only two things: what this person has done with their life and what I stand to gain by listening to them. While some authors write from their observations and opinions, others write from their experiences. There are those who like to think and talk, and there are those who like to roll up their sleeves and do. I tend to have more respect for the latter.

As a teenager, you have a natural nose for hypocrites, liars, frauds and anything that doesn't seem 100% authentic. Your friends are probably pros at talking a good game but not delivering. If you grew up in church, then you probably have seen your fair share of folks that can quote Bible verses like a champ yet their actions often don't match what they preach. They are like religious bobbleheads agreeing with the B ible in word and theory yet their bodies are frozen stiff, unable to live out with any sort of consistency what they believe.

This is nothing new. The church, which is a collection of very broken people, has always struggled in this area because, after all, our bar is Jesus. Although we recognize the life we are called to lead, sin keeps getting in the way. Being like Jesus is something we continually work toward but will never fully achieve in this life. As a teenage Christian, this really bothered me.

Suppose on your next math exam your teacher gives you five problems to solve. You are already panicking because you know if you miss two, you fail. To make matters worse, she tells you that each problem is only worth ten points each and that she would like for you to all get 100s on the test.

What?!?! If the highest possible score is fifty, then how would she expect someone to reach 100?!

This is exactly how I felt when I was introduced to Christianity. I felt as if I was being asked to spend my entire life sacrificing, grinding, loving, serving.... all in an effort to be like someone I could never fully be like!

"This sucks" was a recurring thought I would have growing up in Youth Ministry.

On top of that, questions about whether the Bible was true and trustworthy piled up during my years in college. Eventually I met another Christian who patiently walked me through my doubts and helped me find reasonable, rationale answers to all my questions. After investigating the evidence behind each world religion, it was clear that the claims of Jesus were a thousand times more supported through history, archaeology, prophecy, literature, miracles, science, and the evidence of changed lives than any other theology on Earth.

But just because I accepted Christianity as truth, it didn't mean I was also desiring to follow it.

I had grown up around all of those spiritual smack talkers and few of them impressed me. Church scandals seemed to always fill the evening news. And anytime you saw a Christian in action it appeared they were yelling or shouting at someone in protest. I could roll with Jesus, but the rest of these clowns? Sitting in a pew listening to bad music, trying to stay awake during long winded lectures, being pressured to volunteer, giving 10% of my money to who knows what and having to get up early on the one day of the week I could actually sleep in?

No thanks, I'm good.

That one Christian who I actually got along with in college, who took the time to listen to all my complaints and objections with her faith in God, I ended up marrying her 6 months after graduating. We moved to Austin, TX; bought our first house; and, while she attended church on Sundays, I was out playing basketball with my boys in the neighborhood. Then I experienced something that I had not felt in a very long time. Conviction.

As my wife and I sat out on our porch one evening, we took note of the number of troubled teens that surrounded us. The two teenage boys next door were in and out of juvenile services, battling drug problems, and more. The teens across the street from us were always home but we rarely saw their parents and noise from their wild parties each weekend would keep us up at night. We had met others who lived in nearby low income housing units and were on the brink of foster care.

"The harvest is plentiful, but the workers are few," my wife said.

I knew she was quoting Jesus but I had never really thought about the implications of Jesus' observation in this passage. Could it be that even in Jesus' time there were more thinkers than doers? That there were more religious bobbleheads than there were people of action? Had I become the very thing I had despised? A Christian on paper but an atheist in reality?

The truth is I was a hypocrite trying to avoid other hypocrites. I knew that if I was to step up and attempt to really go all in following Jesus, it was going to be the most difficult process I had ever endured and the 'sanctification' would not end until my life here on Eearth was over. Jesus called it the narrow path.

Despite the temptation to stay complacent, I went all in.

I would spend the next few decades working on the front lines with teens and young adults in ministry. In 2011, I launched an organization called Catalyst Teen Center, now known as the Catalyst Collective. Our mission was to create an environment where every young person could bring their unique purpose to life. What started as a ministry science experiment, continued to grow year after year. As of 2017, Catalyst has connected with and served thousands of students in the Austin area and beyond through after school programs, internships, community service, classes, events, camps, mentoring, and more.

In short, we found the ultimate life hack for teens who earnestly desired insight into how God uniquely made them and why it matters. This book is that hack. The easy path is to remain a normal teen, kinda clueless about what you really have to offer the world and not doing a whole lot that anyone cares about. Or, you can choose to punch normal in the throat by venturing down a narrow path that is filled with great risk and reward.

My prayer is that God awakens within you the very purposes He created you for in this life and beyond.

Joe

YOUR POTENTIAL

Potential is only a measure of what can be, not a measure of what will be. Most of it tends to be wasted, while a fraction of it gets realized. The secret to capturing and fulfilling potential is found piece by piece in each section of this book. The Apostle Paul is a great example of potential that was almost wasted until Jesus not only captured his heart, but taught him how to embrace his unique design. We will continually refer back to Paul and his teachings throughout this journey and provide more detail about his background because God used him to set a standard for how all Christians are to embrace their gifts, talents, passions, and purpose. For now, it's important to note that this is the dude that helped start the first churches all over the Middle East and Europe and wrote most of the letters that make up the New Testament. Much of what we know about what it means to be a Christian comes directly from Paul.

In this section, our goal is to help you evaluate the times we live in, what your role is, and what it will take for you to live a life of meaningful impact. You may feel like just another average teen at times but it's important to note that in God's Kingdom, there is no such thing as average.

CHAPTER 1

THE MODERN INVENTION OF THE TEENAGER

Several years ago I read a book written by two high schoolers that was a catalyst to how I would engage with teens forever. The book was called *Do Hard Things* by Alex and Brett Harris. It was the first time I ever thought to look into the history of how the term "teenager" came about. I'll recap a few things I learned that I hope will be just as eye opening to you as they were to me.

The Invention of the Teen

Let's consider that the concept of a "teen" is still less than 100 years old. The term "teenager" did not even pop into our vocabulary until the 1940s! A brief look at the world of young people from before the time of Jesus to until the early 1900s reveals that two types of human phases existed for almost all of history: children and adults.

In this period of history, you will find no such thing as mandatory public school, career guidance counselors, Little Leagues, or limitations on how old you had to be to hold a job, earn money, or even carry a weapon. Your car was likely a horse and you didn't need a permit, just the ability to not get yourself killed while riding one. By the age of seven, you already knew how to cook, farm, fire a weapon, repair stuff around the house, remedy illnesses or wounds, and take care of infants. By the age of twelve, the world treated you more as an adult than a child and began to talk to you about things like marriage, taking over the family business, and how to defend your home in times of war.

By sixteen or seventeen you were married, or were soon to be married. Drugs and alcohol were legally at your disposal and by the time you reached the now magical age of twenty one, you had the maturity and composure of a modern day forty-year-old. Your youth had well prepared you to be a productive member and leader in society and you were using your skills to produce great stuff for your family and the community around you.

Now let's fast forward to the early 2000s.

By age seven, you were being diagnosed with ADHD for not being able to sit in a chair at school seven hours a day, getting yelled at for not having your helmet on while riding your tricycle around the cul-de-sac, and receiving trophies for coming in dead last in sports. By age twelve, you felt your parents were complete idiots. They couldn't even figure out how to change the ringtone on their phones much less have any wisdom to provide you. You had no choice but to go to school, were too young to get a job, were still seen as a child to the adult world, and had no expectations over you aside from staying out of trouble and getting decent grades.

By sixteen or seventeen, with graduation looming, you were faced with your first adult decision: how to live life on your own. Your parents were not rushing you out of the house so you figured you have another decade before you REALLY need to do the whole 'adulting' thing. Now, you reason, is the time to have some fun, travel, try out college, spend a ton of time with friends and meeting new ones. There's not really a plan, just a confidence that things will all work out and you'll find your path eventually. The world expects little from you and you are happy to live up to the embarrassingly low expectation.

So what happened?

In short, society forgot what young people were capable of. A series of labor and education reform laws in the early 1900s raised the age in which "children" could work and mandated kids stay in school until they were older. The invention of the automobile also meant a teen could travel further to hang out with people, date, and embrace a new kind of independence without carrying as much of the burden to be a productive member in society. Teens became consumers instead of producers. The world adjusted its expectations and wrote you off.

And you loved it.

Action: This will take five minutes, tops. I want you to Google the phrase, "Invention of Teenager" and explore the history on your own. Read at least one article from a legit source on the topic and then share what you learned with someone.

I'm serious, do it.

Your age bracket is enslaved by low expectations and it's going to take young leaders like you who are willing to awaken others to the truth and emancipate them from this tyranny of mediocrity.

CHAPTER 2

THE WORLD WE LIVE IN

What words would you use to describe your generation? Write them here.

The world is changing and to really understand the story we are a part of and the characters within it, we must pull back the camera to look at the big picture.

Truth is, the world described in chapter one a hundred years ago was much, much smaller.

A Global Perspective

So far, your generation is showing signs of some amazing traits. You are the first digitally native generation in history. You grew up with tablets, smartphones and technology next to your sippy cups. This gives you the ability to navigate through a digital landscape faster than any generation before you. You have leveraged this skill to become great storytellers on Instagram, Snapchat and more, but this is only the beginning.

Facebook now has over two billion active users worldwide connecting you to stories, cultures and friends all across the globe. This global community created a generation that embraces diversity like never before. Racism still exists and probably always will until Jesus returns, but your tribe thinks in terms of unity. You love seeing other people come together from different backgrounds for a common good and desire to work toward more of that happening. As global citizens, you have taken a stand against major issues like global poverty, equality, climate change, and war.

You are natural influencers and have used technology and social media to boost your voice, and air your thoughts and opinions, making your mark on the world faster than most of the generations before you ever could.

A Local Perspective

The fact that fifty percent of you come from fatherless homes will be a hard obstacle to overcome, but you will and when you do, you will put in the work to become well-rounded parents. Most forms of authority have failed you—from politicians and police to teachers and pastors who have gotten busted with crazy scandals—but this again, will fuel you to succeed where others have failed.

Not being scared to question tradition has propelled you to new ways of thinking.

You have entrepreneurial DNA running through you that sees ideas for the future and you are willing to risk failure in pursuit of new adventures and endeavors.

While some combo of depression, bullying, and suicide have impacted one in five people your age, it has also sobered you up to the reality that we live in a broken world and something must be done.

Most of your parents are working full time. Schools are overcrowded, making it difficult for teachers and counselors to really get to know you. And mentors are, well, mostly non-existent for people your age. This is driving you to value personal growth and development more than other generations. And with the digital world at your fingertips, you are soaking up knowledge quickly.

And don't let anyone put you down because you're young.
Teach believers with your life: by word, by demeanor,
by love, by faith, by integrity.
1 Timothy 4:12 (MSG)

If you grew up in church, I am sure you have heard this verse a thousand times. Paul wrote it to Timothy, one of the youngest leaders in the Christian church at the time. Timothy embraced leadership at an earlier age than most and was responsible for teaching and leading other new Christians. Knowing what you know now about the invention of the "teen," Paul's words to Timothy here are also his words to you. Isn't it time you make the world remember what you are capable of? Why not let your actions, your character, your belief in the gifts and talents God has given you be the megaphone that captures society's attention once again?

Finish the journey of self discovery we are taking you on in this book and you will have more clarity than ever on what it is you can do to bust out of the slump teenagers have been in for 100 years. We'll say it again—you are capable of way more than you realize!

Before we move into what that looks like specifically for you, there is something we have to talk about: The three biggest influences impacting who you are becoming.

CHAPTER 3

PARENTS, POP CULTURE AND PEERS

What are the biggest influences on a young adult like yourself? Write as many as you can think of here.

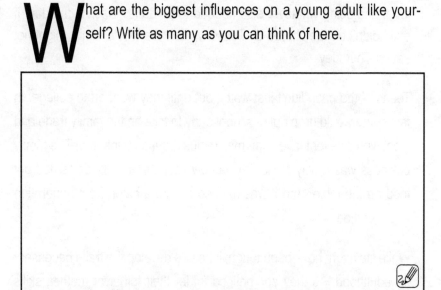

If you look at your life, or the lives of your friends, there are countless factors that have shaped us into who we are and there are countless more that continue to shape us into who we will become.

Out of all of those, none have more power than these three influences: Parents, Pop Culture, and Peers.

Were those on your list?

Hopefully so, it was the title of the chapter. ;) Let's dig deeper...

Parents

From the very beginning, if we look at God's blueprint for influencing the next generation, it centered on the family unit. A beautiful eight pound, six ounce baby was born into a family and for that kid, their family was their life. Starting at a young age, they had an active role to play around the house and there were no free rides. They had expectations and responsibilities that did more than just earn them a gold star on the fridge. They were full time students at the school of Hard Knocks and productive members of the family unit working in the fields, gathering food, and doing whatever else needed to be done. "Back in the day" if a kid didn't do the chores on Tuesday, then the whole family might not eat on Thursday.

Teens of the past didn't just wait it out until they went off to college. In fact some would drop out of school early to take on the family trade and most would never leave a ten mile radius around their home! The family business was a way of life. It was how your dad's dad's dad's dad put food on the table. And it was handed off like a baton from generation to generation.

While life might have been tough, it helped develop the traits necessary for adulthood. As they apprenticed under their father or mother, skills (like how not to die), values, and ultimately identity, were passed on. A kid learned who he was through his father and it was gently nurtured and encouraged through his mother.

Fast forward to Modern America where we are lucky to have one out of two parents at home and we see where this system breaks down pretty quickly. Even the best single parents have to work double time just to put food on the table and are so busy juggling roles as chauffeur, chef, and teacher that counselor can fall down lower on the list. The change in structure has led to a breakdown in the time a parent is able to spend with their child and, consequently, left a generation to parent themselves.

So if your parents aren't at home, then who is "raising" you?

Pop Culture

If some kids have helicopter parents, then my parents had taken off and were on some stealthy mission flying fast and far from home. I remember most days coming home and having the whole house to myself. I'd turn on the TV and ...

...Mr. Feeny was my mentor,

...Saved by the Bell drove my squad goals,

...And the Fresh Prince taught me all I needed to know about becoming an adult.

I was raised by media and, believe it or not, this was before twelve year olds were handed cell phones! Now there are MILLIONS of dollars spent by companies trying to tap into the cell phones you carry with you every day.

Have you ever thought about why they would spend all that money on you? It is almost as if they know these aren't dollars wasted and that if they can just get in front of your mind, a series of internal triggers and dopamine rushes will do the rest. The eyes are the window to the soul, and also to your pocketbooks.

You see media works a little bit like food. We take it in voluntarily: Chew forty times, swallow, consume. And then our body takes over from there, passively doing what it wants with what we take in. In the same way, our mind and spirit passively process what our eyes ingest.

Corporations know this. They know that the media we consume directly translates into action. Obviously they hope it affects what we purchase but even more than that, they hope it shapes our perception of ourselves. What are you wearing? Doesn't this make you feel cool/popular/whatever? What's your style? Do you have the latest and greatest trending _____.

For better or worse, your generation has the whole world at your fingertips. Now the questions is how do you use it as a tool to shape the world and not let it unknowingly shape you?

Peers

"If you are a human, then the biggest influence on your personality is your peer group. Choose your peers. If you want to be better at math, surround yourself with mathematicians. If you want to be more productive, hang out with productive people..."
Mudos Ponens

Or as my mom often yelled it at me: "If you hang out with the chickens, you will learn to cluck. If you hang out with the eagles you will learn to soar."

Name your five closest friends.

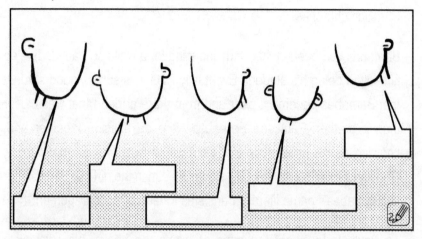

The law of averages say that you are a balance of these five closest friends. Sure you are your own person and every friend group has that "one friend" but what draws you together? You share time, values, advice, and experiences. Together, you celebrate victories and share in struggles. We are made for community. We also learn in community.

Because we share so much of our lives (time and more) with our friends, it is important to look at who we are with and where we are going.

A guy named Tai Lopez created the "Law of 33s." Spend 33% of you time with your peers, 33% with those you can lead/mentor, and 33% with those who can mentor/lead you. Now Paul never saw Tai's Youtube video, but he used this same wisdom to drive his mission.

Paul understood the power of learning under others from a young age getting a Harvard-level education under Gamaliel, a famous Jewish teacher and a powerful politician. After his run in with Jesus, Paul expanded on this training, seeing Jesus as the foretold Jewish messiah and allowing new teachers like Barnabas to teach him to plant new Christian churches.

Barnabas had been at this Christian thing for a while so Paul dedicated himself to being his student. Eventually Paul was such a good student that Barnabas became a peer and from there a friend that was closer than a brother. Paul and Barnabas were on mission together and, knowing all the challenges that Paul would face on his long journey, God knew exactly who to bring alongside him in the difficult times. After all, Barnabas's name literally translates to "son of encouragement"!

As Paul starts to get the hang of things, he begins his own cycle with a young leader named Timothy. Paul didn't have it all figured out but he took notice of Timothy and took him under his wing. He challenged the young man to follow him as he followed Jesus and passed on the same guidance he had received. It is because of this leadership cycle of passing the baton that we are here today.

Action: Take a quick assessment of the people who influence you and those you have the opportunity to influence.

Who is investing into you?

Who are you investing into?

Who is your encourager?

CHAPTER 4

YOUR UNIQUE DESIGN

Hey Snowflake!

I remember the first time my grandma called me a snowflake. Even as a grandma's boy I almost lost my ever loving mind. The term is a low blow meant to show the fragility of the upcoming generation. Agree or disagree, there are many in the older generations that believe that if you are tested you will fall apart. They feel participant ribbons are ridiculous that you need to earn your way like "in the old days."

Hearing the term snowflake come from her lips initially made me want to build a safe space, but here recently I've started to wonder, is being a snowflake really a bad thing?

Snowflakes are unique.

Have you ever thought about what the odds are of you being HERE at this time in history? What are the odds that this ball of dirt and water we call a planet hangs and spins at just the right distance from that mass of perpetual fire we call the sun? What are the odds that it maintains that course and contains all the elements necessary for human life?

One out of nine...er, eight... (sorry Pluto)?

No the odds are much more slim.

What are the odds that human life exists on this planet we call Earth?

Out of all the people throughout history, your family lineage managed to overcome death and disease, predators and pirates, at least long enough to pass on the family genes.

And what are the odds that out of all the people alive today your parents met...and fell in love...and had you? (Love is TOUGH!)

Now if this next part doesn't make any sense you have some extra homework and a long conversation with your parents ahead of you but, you are the result of one particular sperm and one particular egg. Some estimate that the chances of you being the winner of your first race, the one where that one sperm beat out 99.9 million others to meet that one egg of his dreams, are around 1 in 400 quadrillion (Now that's worthy of a ribbon!).

All of that leads to you, with all your unique DNA, born into your unique environment, at a point in history that is like no other!

It takes a lot of math to figure out exactly what the odds of all this occurring are, way more than me and my TI-83 calculator can figure out, but some mathematicians say it is roughly...

One in 10^{2,685,000}

To put that in perspective, the odds of you being alive are about the same as you flipping 30,000 coins and them all landing on their edge, or you being struck by lightning 1.2 thousand times in one day. (Is that lucky or unlucky?)

You are more likely to win the lotto ten times in your life than to even have a life!

Against all odds you are here! Yeah, there is definitely stuff in life, but don't let it overshadow all that you have already overcome just to be here. Because here is the thing, a snowflake by itself might be fragile, but when snowflakes band together, they get stronger.

You get snowballs flying free through the sky or avalanches, movements so powerful that the ground quakes and nothing can stand in their way. That is the power of snowflakes.

You're not here, alive and reading this, at this time by accident. And you're not alone. It's time to join together, punch normal in the throat and bring your unique purposes to life!

The God who made the world and everything in it, this Master of sky and land, doesn't live in custom-made shrines or need the human race to run errands for him, as if he couldn't take care of himself. He makes the creatures; the creatures don't make him. Starting from scratch, he made the entire human race and made the earth hospitable, with plenty of time and space for living so we could seek after God, and not just grope around in the dark but actually find him. He doesn't play hide-and-seek with us. He's not remote; he's near. We live and move in him, can't get away from him!
Acts 17:24-29 (MSG)

CHAPTER 5

SELF AWARENESS

It can be a challenge to appreciate the design of something when you lack an understanding of its parts. Consider the dynamic nature of your smart phone. You are probably discovering new features on it every week with a surprised "I didn't know it could do that" expression on your face. The more time you spend exploring apps and features, the more you unlock it's potential.

It's not much different when it comes to unlocking our potential as God's creation. In fact, I would argue that the very idea of success can be defined by one's ability to take what they have been given in this life (gifts, talents, passions, life experiences etc) and make it all work together toward a common purpose or 'calling'. We will develop this idea more in chapter eleven.

Your level of self awareness is a major factor in foreshadowing the amount of success you may have in this life. If someone asked you today to list a few things you are really good at, how long would it take you to come up with at least ten? At The Catalyst Collective, we have conducted this experiment with teens for years and most cannot list more than five. The few who do list ten take at least five minutes or longer to think about what they are and actually get them on paper.

How long would it take you to list ten features of your smartphone? Bet you could do that in 60 seconds or less! So how is it that we so easily analyze things around us more effectively than we analyze ourselves?

One observation is that we are creatures of necessity. We don't like to do anything we don't HAVE to do. As a teen, you get up in the morning because you HAVE to go to school. You make or buy your lunch because you HAVE to eat. You turn in assignments only when they HAVE to be graded. Self awareness, on the other hand, does not make the daily chore list of things you HAVE to be or do. It's not a necessity.

So what is the motivation for investing in self awareness? Why go through an entire book on it?

We could give you a top ten list here but the most important reason is this: **Lives depend on it.**

There are many times in the New Testament where we see Paul's anger flare up over the blatant disrespect and neglect Christians were having for the gifts God gave them. In his letter to the Corinthian church, he called out one grievance specifically: sexual immorality. He had this to say:

Or didn't you realize that your body is a sacred place, the place of the Holy Spirit? Don't you see that you can't live however you please, squandering what God paid such a high price for? The physical part of you is not some piece of property belonging to the spiritual part of you. God owns the whole works. So let people see God in and through your body.
1 Corinthians 6:17-20 (MSG)

Paul's response here is not aimed at addressing only the sin of sexual immorality but the underlying sin of taking all that God has created us with and using it for selfish gain. Jesus' life on Earth was a dividing line in history. No longer could mankind pretend that we didn't know who God was or why He created us. Jesus was sent on the greatest rescue mission of all time and before He left he commissioned us to pick up where He left off.

It would take a few decades after Jesus' death before we would realize that He didn't just commission us, He equipped us! He gave us a heads up on the Holy Spirit and the spiritual gifts that would follow but we had forgotten about our natural talents, our passions, our personality types, our life experiences and so much more that, like our fingerprints, would set us individually apart and yet weave together a unique design that was meant to reflect God in all that we set out to do.

Leveraging what we had been given to love God and love others was the mission. In so doing, we would teach others about who God is, why we are here and where we are headed while doing our best to model God's character in our actions. The lives of those around the world who did not yet know their Creator were depending on it.

With a revived focus, insight from the Holy Spirit, and a mission that was bigger than any one person could bear, we were empowered to use our giftings as Christ's representatives to awaken a world that had lost its understanding as to why we were ever created in the first place.

So of all the things we HAVE to do as humans to survive, self aware-ness may not be something we get out of bed thinking about each morning, but it is the compass that guides our path, helps determine our steps, and aligns us with the purposes God created us for.

There will always be those people who hold a smartphone in their hands and yet use it only to make phone calls while the rest of its powerful potential lies dormant. I can think of no greater regret or disappointment than to have lived a full life here on Earth only to find out in the end that I only used five percent of my God-given potential to make a difference in the lives of others.

I'm perfectly fine with making mistakes but failing to invest in the discovery and application of my unique design is not one of them. There is simply too much at stake.

SECTION 2

YOUR DESIGN

Things are about to get a little heavy. Your individual design is intricate and to understand it effectively, you have to be willing to study it in parts. We will help you begin to connect the pieces at the end of this section but you have to put in the work to take each exercise seriously. Rush through these chapters and you might as well take that bucket of potential and toss it in trash.

Our goal over the next five chapters is to help you gain a level of self awareness that will set you up for recognizing your purpose or calling with clarity. You are about to go to war against normal and we've got your back. Let's get started.

CHAPTER 6

PUZZLE PIECE #1 LIFE EXPERIENCES

There is no denying our life experiences shape us; Sometimes positively, sometimes negatively - sometimes both. Our past can toughen us up, make us wiser, inspire change or it can instill fear, create emotional scars and prevent us from trusting others or taking risks. Allow me to give you an example from my life and from the life of Paul before you turn to look at how your own life experiences may be shaping you.

I always hated going to church growing up. By the time I reached high school, I could see the light at the end of the tunnel. No, not the light of Jesus. The light of finally getting confirmed in the Catholic church and being done with this whole Sunday school/youth group thing for good. I had met every requirement asked of me from 1st grade on, with one exception. I was required to go on two church camp retreats and I had only attended one. As a result, the church I had grown up in told me I could not be confirmed in my faith and shipped me across town to a different church that was only requiring their students to attend one camp retreat.

It was at this point that my skepticism of the validity of church and it's leaders took root. I was pissed. All I wanted to do was get this church thing over with, appease my parents and get on with my life.

A few years later in college, I would reopen the door to my faith and explore the validity of the Christianity, as well as other religions, on my own. What God did during that time was miraculous. I did, eventually, make my Christian faith my own, despite my distaste for the institutional church. However, giving my life to Jesus and being around more Christians made things harder, not easier.

The first Bible study on campus I decided to attend was terrible. It had nothing to do with the teaching. That part I'm sure would have been great—had anyone else decided to show up! "Typical Christians," I thought to myself, always saying one thing and doing another. I would go on to watch Christians show up to Bible studies and talk a good game, then go get drunk and live like everyone else was living.

The first church I attended after graduating from college ended in scandal with the senior pastor caught stealing half a million dollars from the ministry.

On my first youth retreat as a leader, I experienced the one thing every ministry worker and parent fears the most: a student dying. A young lady, who was a visitor on the trip, tragically drowned in the lake where we were camping. The whole church was devastated and nearly closed its doors for good. I took a step back from serving at the time, but God would not let me stay on the bench for long. I would jump back in months later and spend the next several years dealing with the unending punches of parents who didn't like my leadership, teaching, song selection, and everything else that didn't fit into the mold of what they wanted for their son or daughter.

Eight years removed from becoming a Christian in college and I finally embraced two key truths that would set me up for long term success:

1. **Working or serving in the church is not for the weak**. People don't automatically become like Jesus when they choose to follow Him. You still encounter ungratefulness, rudeness, gossip, slander, the difficulty of establishing great friendships that dissipate over time, being taken advantage of, criticism, and serving other brothers and sisters who would rather point out everything that is broken and needs fixing than roll up their sleeves and help. But.....

2. **I was not weak**. My life experiences of being let down by my fellow Christians toughened me up. I was not only made to handle the adversity of ministry, I was made to lead others through it as well.

Let's briefly consider another example from Paul's life experiences. His zeal (passion) for God took root at an early age as a child being deeply trained in the Old Testament scriptures and knowing how to uphold Jewish law and traditions. He was a Roman citizen with exposure to many different cultures and languages. History reveals Paul to be a great teacher, decisive decision maker, good delegator, a man of action, bold and encouraging. Willing to die for a cause, that's the kind of courage he had. A passion for justice and truth ran through him with the ability to take his theological training and articulate it into writings the common, uneducated person could understand.

Now if that were the opening paragraph to Paul's resume, I would put him at the top of the list of candidates to lead a new church movement, wouldn't you? Well, Jesus did. And once Paul accepted the job, his experiences would help forge him into one of the greatest leaders in history. In this passage, we get some insight into what it was like for Paul to bring the gospel to new parts of the world. While many would have let stuff like this break them, Paul let this adversity develop his resolve to continue down the narrow path he was made for.

I've worked much harder, been jailed more often, beaten up more times than I can count, and at death's door time after time. I've been flogged five times with the Jews' thirty-nine lashes, beaten by Roman rods three times, pummeled with rocks once. I've been shipwrecked three times, and immersed in the open sea for a night and a day. In hard traveling year in and year out, I've had to ford rivers, fend off robbers, struggle with friends, struggle with foes. I've been at risk in the city, at risk in the country, endangered by desert sun and sea storm, and betrayed by those I thought were my brothers. I've known drudgery and hard labor, many a long and lonely night without sleep, many a missed meal, blasted by the cold, naked to the weather.

And that's not the half of it...

2 Corinthians 11:23-28 (MSG)

In a similar fashion to these examples, God is forging you, through some of your own life experiences, into a person who can handle the adversity of a narrow road uniquely made for you. No matter what path you take in life, whether it strays from God or not, there is no avoiding difficulty, hardship, and pain. We live in a broken world and until Jesus returns, life is gonna suck at times. This does not, however, give us a license to be angry, bitter, justify our sin or hide under a rock. Instead it should be our wake up call that this life is not what we were made for - there is more! God has a knack of redeeming every bad thing we have ever experienced, if we let Him.

On the flip side, our positive life experiences are equally as valuable in shaping who we become and how we live. It's important that we evaluate what has gone right in life and why it's meaningful to us. This next exercise is designed to help you account for both the positive and negative experiences you have had on Earth so far. After completing this activity, you will have your first, significant piece in your hand to the puzzle of your unique design and perhaps some general ideas on how all of this may give you a glimpse into what's ahead.

Action: Let's start with the positive. Starting from childhood and working up to where you are today, reflect on the people, circumstances, events, or experiences that made a positive impact on you. Depending on how good your memory is (mine is terrible) you could probably list lots of examples, so try to focus on the experiences you often think back on, how they impacted you in the past and could still be having a positive impact on you today.

Examples may include specific mentors, teachers, or coaches that encouraged and led you well, something you achieved or won, somewhere you traveled, or someone you served. If it meant a lot to you, write it down and note why it was meaningful.

Now it's time to do the same reflecting over the negative experiences in our life. For many of us this is a road we would rather not travel back down, yet it is vital to the process of becoming self-aware. If doing this begins to stir up some unsettling emotional memories, we highly encourage you to talk to a counselor or adult you trust about it. Keeping past pains bottled up never plays out well and can ultimately prevent you from embracing who you were born to be.

As you think through the people, events, and choices that have had a negative impact on your life, you might already see how that adversity has been leveraged in a positive way. For now, though, just take note of things that did negatively impact you at some point in life.

CHAPTER 7

PUZZLE PIECE #2
SPIRITUAL GIFTS

As we mentioned in the intro section of this book which we know you were tempted to skip but didn't, we are tracking the life and teachings God delivered through the Apostle Paul to help us sort out our unique design. As we do, there are a few things that you need to know about big P.

For starters, the dude was WELL educated. Some generations grew up in church learning cute songs and small verses in the Bible. Coloring pages and Veggietales was their curriculum. Not for Paul. From a young age he studied under rabbis and developed a deep passion to uphold the Jewish law. In fact, he probably knew more about theology by the age of thirteen than most of today's Bible college graduates.

Paul also did not start out as one of the good guys. Because of the mindset of many Jews at the time, he learned to despise all people and customs that were not of Jewish descent (the Bible calls them Gentiles). They were seen as a contamination to God's ways and to God's people. By the time Paul hits his late twenties and early thirties (he was about the same age as Jesus), he begins hearing about this new prophet-teacher-rabbi guy named Jesus who has been disturbing the peace with his ideas on how to interpret the Old Testament Scripture.

Jesus was doing miracles, dropping knowledge bombs left and right, making Paul's crew (the Pharisees) look like fools and had some very harsh, public criticism regarding the way guys like Paul are leading the Jewish people. Men and women of all cultures, Jew and Gentile alike, were beginning to love this new message from Jesus (called the Gospel) and were questioning the Jewish leadership that had been in power for centuries.

This didn't go over too well with zealots like Paul, so by the time of Jesus' death and resurrection, when Jesus' followers who would become known as Christians began to emerge, Paul was tasked with destroying this movement before it could spread further. When Jesus eventually confronted Paul in Acts 9 we see the beginning to one of the most radical conversions in history. Paul was not brainwashed, in case you are wondering. He was enlightened. For the next decade, Paul would, in a way, go back to Bible college and learn how to make sense of the Old Testament in light of Jesus' teachings. The letters he would write to early church communities would go on to make up most of the New Testament.

The hate and pride in Paul's heart was replaced with love, compassion, and humility. He went on to discover the unique design God had given him - how his life experiences, natural talents, passions, personality, spiritual gifts, and more would work together to put him in a position to expand the early church throughout the Middle East and parts of Europe.

This is all background and set up for one of my favorite sections from Paul, which is his teachings on spiritual gifts. In his letter to the church in Corinth, he explains the dynamic of spiritual gifts and how they should be used. I'll explain here and skip around a bit, but you can go back and read the whole chapter if you want. It's awesome.

God's various gifts are handed out everywhere; but they all originate in God's Spirit. God's various ministries are carried out everywhere; but they all originate in God's Spirit. God's various expressions of power are in action everywhere; but God Himself is behind it all. Each person is given something to do that shows who God is: Everyone gets in on it, everyone benefits. All kinds of things are handed out by the Spirit, and to all kinds of people! The variety is wonderful:

wise counsel

clear understanding

simple trust

healing the sick

miraculous acts

proclamation

distinguishing between spirits

tongues

interpretation of tongues

All these gifts have a common origin, but are handed out one by one by the one Spirit of God. He decides who gets what, and when. I want you to think about how all this makes you more significant, not less.

A body isn't just a single part blown up into something huge. It's all the different-but-similar parts arranged and functioning together. If Foot said, "I'm not elegant like Hand, embellished with rings; I guess I don't belong to this body," would that make it so? If Ear said, "I'm not beautiful like Eye, limpid and expressive; I don't deserve a place on the head," would you want to remove it from the body? If the body was all eye, how could it hear? If all ear, how could it smell? As it is, we see that God has carefully placed each part of the body right where he wanted it.
1 Corinthians 12: 4-11; 14-18 (MSG)

You know how excited you get right before someone opens a really great gift you got them that you know they will love? That's how I imagine Paul feeling as he writes about how the Holy Spirit has intentionally, specifically given each of us gifts that are to be used to reveal a piece of God to the world.

Now imagine what it would feel like if that same person was not only unenthusiastic about opening your gift but decided to hand it right back to you with a polite and brief, "No thank you."

I can't tell you what God must be thinking or feeling when, as His creation, we don't take the time to learn about the gifts we have been given nor how to use them, but I can tell you it's not wise for us to do this. Why would we want to dismiss such a vital part of our being here on Earth?

Action: You may have taken a test similar to this in the past, but if it has been longer than six months, we encourage you to do it again. Here are a few free spiritual gifts tests we recommend. You can also search online for "Free Spiritual Gifts Test for Teens" and find a different one.

- www.spiritualgiftstest.com —This is a great one with adult and student versions.
- www.teensundayschool.com/122/activities/spiritual-gifts-analysis.php —This is the fastest one to get through and covers the most common gifts. We use this one at camps a bunch.
- www.giftstest.com —This one is the most in depth, covering all the gifts, but will take a little longer to complete.

When you are finished, record your top three Spiritual Gifts in the space below.

Finally, flip to Appendix A in the back of this book to read a little more about how your top three spiritual gifts are designed to impact those around you.

CHAPTER 8

PUZZLE PIECES #3 AND #4 NATURAL TALENTS AND FIVE WORDS

I want you to imagine: there you are in class eagerly awaiting the bell while being reminded to take seriously the upcoming exam as you scurry to pack your stuff together. Then your teacher let's out this deep sigh, and slightly rolls her eyes when she hears one of your classmates ask when the test will be. Never mind that it's written on the board, on the study guide, was emailed to you and your parents a week ago, and announced three times in class since.

You think to yourself, "How can anyone be THAT clueless??"

At lunch you find yourself in the middle of a conversation that turned very serious and deep when the topic of suicide came up. One of your friends, who rarely opens up, begins to be vulnerable about their own experience attempting suicide. You and your friends are shocked and saddened because you never would have guessed someone like this would struggle with depression at all, let alone suicide. Your shock turns to anger when someone three seats down, eavesdropping of course, blurts out "Ah, that's nothing. I knew a guy once who actually went through with it." Your friend across from you, ignoring the extremely rude and brash comment that was just made chimes in with "Ya ok, how about we change the subject? I don't like talking about depressing stuff like this."

You think to yourself, "WOW, how can these people be so insensitive and self absorbed?!"

Later that same afternoon, you get forced into playing dodgeball in gym - guys vs girls. You figure that if you have to play then you are playing to win. Your team does not share your same conviction as they joke around the whole time trying to be the first ones to get knocked out. The other team is now trash talking which makes your blood boil. You want to single handedly take them on all by yourself to shut them up.

You think to yourself, "Why does nobody seem to care about winning and why do I hate losing so much?"

There are situations like these that go on all throughout the day that are like windows of insight into how we are each designed. The clueless classmate is not stupid, they just don't have the talent of organization like you do. The conversation at lunch reveals that you not only have a knack to read people and situations, but that you are a great listener with tons of compassion and may have a gift for counseling others rising inside you. It's just a stupid game of dodgeball but it does bring to the surface your competitive nature and your drive to do things with excellence.

Could it be that God designed many of these attributes in you for a reason?

We often get so distracted by the talents we don't have that is prevents us from using the ones that we do have. Several thousand years ago Moses was faced with many leadership tasks that he was either not equipped to handle by himself or lacked to faith to do, but God had his back. He provided Moses a brother who was his public speaker, a father-in-law who taught him how to delegate and ton of people in the community like this dude, Bezalel, who was key in constructing the tabernacle.

God spoke to Moses: "See what I've done; I've personally chosen Bezalel son of Uri, son of Hur of the tribe of Judah. I've filled him with the Spirit of God, giving him skill and know-how and expertise in every kind of craft to create designs and work in gold, silver, and bronze; to cut and set gemstones; to carve wood—he's an all-around craftsman.
Exodus 31:1-5 (MSG)

God knew what He was doing when He designed you. Add that to the fact that He even knew what time period you would be born in and which part of the world you would impact (Acts 17:26). I think it's safe to say that God cares deeply about the choices you make with the gifts, talents, and time on Earth that He has given you. As a teenager, you have an amazing opportunity to do something most adults you know are still trying to figure out - how to identify and target talent.

Let's continue dissecting your unique design with some exercises that we hope you will not rush through.

Action: You are going to need a partner for this one - someone who knows you well. Don't try to cheat yourself by not getting someone else involved in this either.

Here is where our doubt flares up. We think we are good at something, but we're not really sure. We have hunches, but not confidence. This is not the time to be humble, though. If you think you might have a talent for something, write it down. If you suck at it, that's why you got a friend involved to tell you.

On the flip-side, your friend may also make you list things that they think you are good at, but you don't think you are. Write it down, if they tell you to. You can put a question mark by it if it will make you feel better.

It can seem incredibly difficult to try and think of even ten things to put down here but the truth is God has already gifted you with hundreds of talents. Most of them are going unrecognized because you figure everyone can do it, too, so it's nothing special. There will always be talents that seem common because they are shared by many but the goal here is to identify what your unique mix of natural talent looks like and by the end of this section, how it might be targeted.

Exercise 1 - Natural Talent Inventory

Before you start, remember that a natural talent is just something that comes naturally to you. You can do it without a ton of effort. It could be a skill like fixing specific things, singing, acting, and writing. It could be more descriptive in nature, like listening, empathy, or patience. Think about any time someone has ever said "WOW, You are good at _____" and write it down.

Don't stop until you have listed twenty items. Then, circle the top five that you feel most confident in.

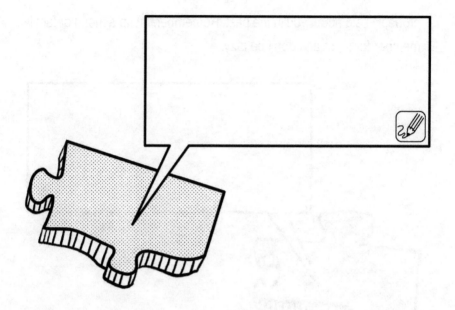

Good.

Make sure you circled the top five talents that you feel are your strongest, or could be your strongest. If you wrote a list without a friend's involvement, stop and send them this text:

"Hey. I'm doing this assignment thing and it's making me ask a friend what my natural talents are. Here is the list I came up with. Which do you think are my strongest? Would you add anything I missed?"

Since that wasn't hard, let's keep the momentum going...

Exercise 2 - Words That Describe You

Again, with a friend's input, write down twenty words that you feel describe who you are. Things like fast learner, nurturing, counselor, loyal, outgoing, positive, etc. These are things that other people have probably said about you in the past. Remember, hit up a friend or family member for input and don't be lazy.

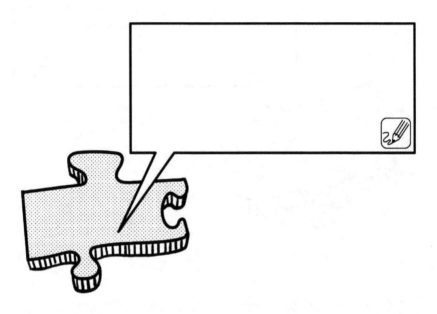

So now we have two lists with a total of ten things circled.

In our final box, it's time to look at these ten circled descriptors of yourself and list what they have in common. Do you see any common themes? How could some of these skills and traits work together to impact others?

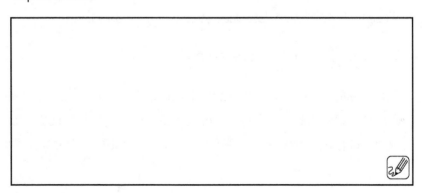

CHAPTER 9

PUZZLE PIECE #5 PASSIONS

This topic will either get you stirred up or frustrated. My wife hates it because she feels like she never has an answer that is as good as someone else's. The good news is you can't get this part wrong. Give me a few minutes to frame this up before we jump into it.

It's important to not confuse passion with infatuation. A passion is a strong desire to do something that is more long lived and is something that you are willing to endure some adversity over. Infatuation on the other hand, is short lived and is not something you will generally sacrifice much for. Shows on Netflix, crushes, great books or stories, new apps on your phone, video games....these are all things that you can get infatuated with. And no, sacrificing sleep to binge watch *Stranger Things* does not qualify as a passion.

Remember Paul's list of stuff he went through (from Chapter Six) in bringing the Gospel to new cultures? That's passion. You can catch a glimpse of what passion looks like in all his letters. Take, for example, this message he had for the church in Philippi.

Yes, all the things I once thought were so important are gone from my life. Compared to the high privilege of knowing Christ Jesus as my Master, firsthand, everything I once thought I had going for me is insignificant—dog dung. I've dumped it all in the trash so that I could embrace Christ and be embraced by him. I didn't want some petty, inferior brand of righteousness that comes from keeping a list of rules when I could get the robust kind that comes from trusting Christ— God's righteousness. I gave up all that inferior stuff so I could know Christ personally, experience his resurrection power, be a partner in his suffering, and go all the way with him to death itself.
Philippians 3:7-11 (MSG)

These are the words of someone who has developed a passion for a cause and is willing to go the distance to champion it. As we turn to consider some things you may have a passion for you need to know that it's TOTALLY FINE if your passions are not as fully formed as Paul's.

We can all agree that this world is a broken place. Injustice is everywhere. So one purpose of the passion question aims to draw out which parts of this broken world stir in you the most. It might seem a tad cold if I were to tell you I care more about you discovering your gifts and passions than I do about homelessness in America but I'm just not as excited to serve the poor as I am to equip you to serve the poor - should that be one of your passions. It would be foolish to compare passions or causes with others. Doing that would negate God's design as well as all of these other puzzle pieces that make us unique.

Passions do not always relate to some big injustice in the world either. Having a positive life experience with a teacher or coach growing up could inspire a passion in you to become one some day. Identifying what inspires you to action in this life is so important. In fact, go ahead and take an inventory of anything that has ever inspired you and list why it inspired you.

I know some of you would love to play professional sports. Some would love to own their own business, be a pilot, actor, make movies, etc. These are all things that you have been inspired by at some point.

Don't stop until you think through seven examples.

Now before you answer this next question in the action section, there are 3 rules you need to follow:

Rule #1: When we say "unlimited time," you are still bound to our 24-hour day. So, you couldn't fight every single injustice on earth, but you could make a serious dent in one particular area, especially when combined with all the money and resources you need.

Rule #2: Don't answer with your head. Answer with your heart. Yes, access to clean water may be one of the largest problems our planet faces, but that may not necessarily be an issue you are super passionate about and that's perfectly fine. Are you passionate about being the first person to land on Mars? That counts, write it down.

Rule #3: Review your life experiences. It may not be the case for you, but for many, our greatest pains do foreshadow our greatest passions. Consider how your experiences in life have influenced issues that matter to you in this world.

Action: **Passion Question:** If you were given unlimited time, money, and resources, what would you do to make this world a better place?

Write down a few areas that come to mind. What issue would you tackle? In what part of the world? What age group? Try to be specific and remember that some passions may not relate to an injustice. If you have a passion for fixing and refurbishing cars, you are very much using your talents to make this world a better place.

Perhaps you have a history of cancer in your family and that is an area you are passionate about seeing others find comfort and healing in? That's a good start but whom, what types of cancer and where might you start? That's being specific.

Now for some final self-reflection: Look at everything you wrote down in this chapter, and take note of any recurring themes, connections or anything that stands out to you. Maybe your answers all involve working with people. Perhaps many of your answers relate to building or creating things. The possibilities are endless.

Go ahead and light a cigar and grab your detective hat. Text a friend for help, too, if needed.

We are about to help you pull all this together, so hang on!

(Oh, and just kidding about the cigar. We hear smoking is frowned upon for teens.)

CHAPTER 10

PUTTING SOME PIECES TOGETHER

At this point, we have five of our nine pieces framed up: Life experiences, spiritual gifts, natural talents, five words that most describe you, and passions. Great work so far!! It's time to zoom back out and take a look at the big picture. Let's go back through the answers you gave in this section, and follow the directions to summarize everything on the puzzle we provided here.

The thing about puzzles is that everyone goes into solving them with a strategy. We start with the border, sort the colors, have the box cover close as a reference and pick a section to start in. Ironically, when it comes to solving the puzzle of who we are and what we are designed to do in this life, we execute only a fraction of the strategy that we use in solving these simple, meaningless box puzzles. Talk about injustice!

As we wrap up Section Two, you have created a border around your purpose and sorted everything into sections. The problem is you don't have the box cover, just the pieces ready to be connected, so let's connect some pieces.

Action: Connecting the pieces is a three step process:

Step 1: Fill out your answers from the previous chapters (6-9) and look for connections.

A connection is something in one of your pieces that fits together with something in a different piece. For example, let's say you have the spiritual gift of exhortation or encouragement, the natural talents of listening and problem solving and passion to work with children in the foster care system. Those are three great connections which look to me like the potential makings of a great counselor who will know when to listen, encourage and guide!

Maybe public speaking is a natural talent. You have the spiritual gift of evangelism and a passion to travel. Those are three great connections that could point to you preaching the gospel as a missionary around the world!

Put back on your detective hat. If these were all clues to solving the mystery of what your specific purpose can look like, what stands out to you? Remember, there is NO SINGLE CORRECT ANSWER. The only way to know for sure will be to pick a direction and begin walking down it. (We will cover that later).

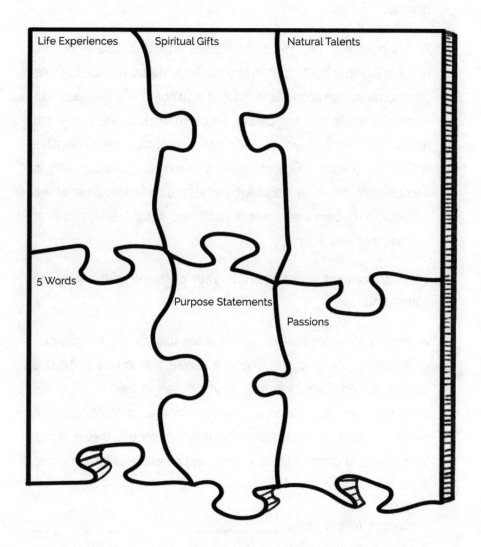

Step 2: Draw a line between connections you see and look for themes.

At this point you may see some themes emerging. Like writing an essay, a theme is the main idea of something. Maybe you see that one thing some of your connections have in common is that they deal with interacting face to face with people. If so, then 'working one on one with people' is a theme. Maybe you see that creativity is a theme because writing, art, building things or inventing is something that appears in your pieces consistently. This begins to set you up for step three where we would ask about what kinds of things you would create, and what purpose they would serve.

Step 3: Connect your themes to your passions with a purpose statement.

In drawing some conclusions, you may see that you are a highly creative person, who enjoys dealing with people face to face and has a passion to help them overcome traumatic pain in their life. Possible areas of purpose could lie in Art Therapy, Counseling, teaching under-privileged youth, or doing something new that nobody else is doing. Your goal is to connect these themes and passions using a purpose statement like this:

"I can see myself doing _____ for _____, because I would be excited to see _____."

Specific Examples:

I can see myself <u>teaching guitar</u> for <u>kids in poverty</u>, because I would be excited to see <u>them have the opportunity to explore and develop a skill that they normally could not afford to pay for.</u>

I can see myself <u>starting a 24-7 teen center</u> for <u>all teens</u>, because I would be excited to see <u>them have access to people who care about who they are and where they are going personally, professionally and spiritually.</u>

I can see myself <u>getting involved in student council</u>, because I would be excited to see <u>every student have the best possible experience socially and academically in school.</u>

Take some time to think through a few purpose statements of your own and write down at least three in the space provided. Your purpose statements will fall into one of these categories:

1. Something completely new you have never done before

2. Something kinda new but similar to what you have done or are doing

3. Something that is a bigger step down the path you are already on

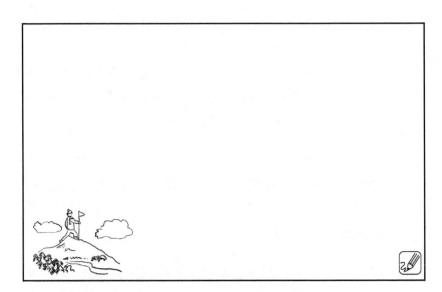

Consider this a first draft at discovering some of your unique purposes. I want to tell you that the vast majority of people on this planet never even get this far in the pursuit of their unique purpose.

YOU ARE DOING GREAT!

If you are not happy with the purpose statements you have crafted or having trouble thinking of what they might be, we have a few options for you:

1. Show five people your puzzle overview from this exercise and ask for their input on what connections and themes they see.

2. Consider taking advantage of a thirty-minute or one-hour coaching session with our team. We will look at what you have written down so far, ask you a bunch of questions and help you think through possible purpose statements. To learn more about our coaching sessions, go to www.throatpunchnormal.com.

SECTION 3

YOUR CALLING

If you took your time through Section Two, then there are probably a ton of thoughts, questions and ideas bouncing around your mind. Having too many passions can feel paralyzing because it's hard to know which one to focus on, while having too few can make you question if something is broken within you.

In Section Three, we will address the paranoia that some have around the idea of a calling and add a few more pieces to the mix as we take a step back to evaluate your work so far. Keep the momentum going and do not give up. Answers are coming.

CHAPTER 11

DO I HAVE A CALLING?

E very denomination of Christianity seems to have a slightly different take on the idea of a 'calling'. For some it is a supernatural event where clear direction is given from God on a particular action or vocation. Some believe the concept is over spiritualized and would argue that a calling is just a religious expression describing one's passion or gut instinct when choosing a direction to go. What we can all agree on is that God is the one who gave us the ability to have passion and the freedom to make our own choices to begin with. While God can and does give clear signs when directing us, this is not always the case. For this reason we will use a more conservative definition of the word 'calling'.

> Calling (*Noun*) - a strong urge toward a particular
> way of life or career; a vocation.

With that out of the way, let us introduce you to two types of 'callings': General and Specific.

Our general calling focuses on the fact that we have an inward desire to know where we come from, and where we are going. This desire to know where we came from and why we are here on Earth was put within us by a Creator and is designed to draw us down the path of discovering who this Creator is, and what He wants from us.

He has made everything beautiful in its time.
He has also set eternity in the human heart; yet no one can fathom
what God has done from beginning to end.
Ecclesiastes 3:11 (NIV)

As Christians, we believe our general calling is summed up in the two greatest commandments: To love God and love others. For someone who is not a Christian, their general calling might simply be "doing good" in this life.

The question we are really asking when discussing this topic deals not so much with our general calling but our specific calling as we explore what it is we may have been uniquely born to do.

This, however, is where the concept of a specific calling breaks down and gets confusing. Most of us fear having this mystical calling in our life that God intended for us to fulfill and because we didn't read the signs correctly, we totally missed it.

What if you were meant to be a doctor, lawyer, actor, politician, etc., but either never had the chance to pursue it or missed your opportunity all together? What if God has been throwing signs at you left and right and you are just not seeing them? What if you think you know what you are supposed to do but are too afraid to do it?

If that resonates with you, take a deep breath - we have good news! There is so much paranoia about getting this stuff wrong that we get blinded to the bigger picture which is that the only way you can miss your specific calling in life is *by doing nothing at all*. Let's look at why this is the case.

Can a supernatural being, such as God, step in and assign a specific task to us? As we already mentioned, the answer is Yes! The Bible, for example, was written by average, imperfect people who were given a specific task to record events in history. However, just because this kind of thing does happen, it doesn't mean it's supposed to happen for <u>everyone</u>.

The Apostle Paul wrote to the early churches in Rome and Corinth and took time in the 12th chapter of each letter to help the members of the community at the time understand their specific role. And guess what? These specific roles or 'callings' were directional, informative...and yet, pretty vague at the same time.

We learn we have a unique mix of natural and spiritual gifts that are designed to be used in collaboration with others' gifts to make a difference in the world around us. We also learn that we are given freedom to take our gifts and go meet the needs we encounter. The choice of what to do, how to do it, and when to do it is left to us!

This all equates to a tremendous amount of freedom to go reflect the character of God by creating and being the individuals He uniquely created us to be. If we decide to squander our natural talents, spiritual gifts, passions, etc. by not using them to serve others or reflect God's beauty, then we have in fact missed our 'calling' to be His ambassadors here on Earth. To summarize:

YES, you have a general calling as God's creation to love Him and love others.

YES, you have freedom to use the gifts God has given you to make an impact in the world.

Or to put it from the Apostle Paul's perspective:

It is absolutely clear that God has called you to a free life. Just make sure that you don't use this freedom as an excuse to do whatever you want to do and destroy your freedom. Rather, use your freedom to serve one another in love; that's how freedom grows. For everything we know about God's Word is summed up in a single sentence: Love others as you love yourself. That's an act of true freedom. If you bite and ravage each other, watch out—in no time at all you will be annihilating each other, and where will your precious freedom be then? My counsel is this: Live freely, animated and motivated by God's Spirit.
Galatians 5:13-16 (MSG)

This freedom gives you the ability to pursue many specific callings over your lifetime. Some may last for a short season while others could remain for decades. Those who tend to find their niche and excel in it are those that have developed a strong self awareness and, spiritually speaking, have maintained a consistent relationship with God in prayer and study of Scripture. By going through this book you are developing those self awareness muscles which will help you feel more confident about the actions you decide to take.

Just remember that the only way to miss out on the things God has for you is to remain complacent, acquiring knowledge about the Bible but doing nothing with it. Instead, take whatever you do know about God and yourself today and do something with it. If all you knew about God was that He loves to comfort those in pain and all you knew about yourself is that you are a great listener, then take those two truths and look for opportunities to comfort those going through some hard things by being that friend who listens, doesn't judge, and empathizes with the pain of others. In so doing you will find yourself right in the middle of fulfilling one of many specific purposes God has for your life.

Action: When we combine our gifts and talents with areas that we are passionate about, we find ourselves in a place where we are maximizing our potential to express God's character and impact the world around us. This exercise is designed to get you thinking further about your potential passions which we talked about in the last section. To follow the definition of the term 'calling' as outlined, we will think of a potential calling in the simple form of an urge.

You might have watched a show on Netflix about a detective and had the urge to be a crime scene investigator as a result. Did that urge stick around well after the show? Did that urge surface again and again at other times? Maybe you had the urge to go sit with someone at lunch who always looks lonely or sad? Each day you see the same student in the corner by himself and every time you do that urge resurfaces. Urges can lead to big or small actions. Try to identify at least seven of the most consistent urges you have had no matter how random they seem.

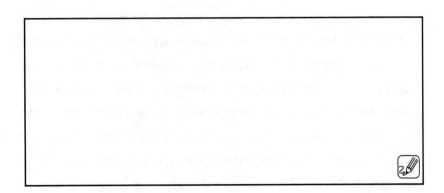

CHAPTER 12

PUZZLE PIECE #6 PERSONALITY TYPE

"Your vision will become clear only when you can look into your own heart. Who looks outside, dreams; who looks inside, awakes."
– Carl Jung

Carl Gustav Jung was a Swiss psychiatrist and psychotherapist who founded analytical psychology. His work has been influential, not only in psychiatry, but also in philosophy, anthropology, archaeology, literature, and religious studies. His research would later provide the foundation for one of the world's most widely used and scientifically verified personality assessments known as the Myers-Briggs Type Indicator or MBTI.

It's totally fine if you don't know what half the words in that first paragraph mean. We had to look some up ourselves. This personality test based on Jung's work is not a test to see which *Star Wars* character you are. This is an exercise in further self-awareness which is the key to unlocking your true potential in life.

For most of my teens and twenties I carried a very low self image. I always felt average at everything. I would be inspired to start projects but never finish them. Whether I was at work or school I would inwardly critique the decisions my bosses or teachers were making, thinking I could do the job better myself if given the opportunity - but I never was. I hated my introverted (shy) nature and wished I was more outgoing. I had big ideas yet no room to do anything about them. I felt worthless and stuck for so long.

This test I am about to ask you to take was a catalyst for me. It opened my eyes to things I always felt but didn't know how to put in words. It helped me connect so many dots about how I was wired and how it all works together to make me unique. With better understanding of myself came greater confidence to do the things I knew I was capable of. For this reason and many more, I am going to ask you to invest the time to take this test yourself and reading up on your personality type afterwards.

It's ok to be skeptical. My first reaction to these types of things was not positive. I remember thinking, "where does the Bible talk about personality types anyway?" Then I heard a famous speaker say once that the Bible doesn't talk about a ton of things that are real, like polar bears, for example. It's not an encyclopedia. That was a good point. The Apostle Paul might have very well been an ENTJ type, which doesn't mean anything to you at the moment but if you share that same personality type you might find it interesting.

Since this section takes a little more time than normal to complete and, in our opinion, vital to the overall identification of your unique purposes, we will conclude our thoughts here and jump into how to take this test.

Action: At this point, we would like for you to visit www.16personalities. com to take a free MBTI assessment. You can also search online for "free myers briggs test" but 16 Personalities is our favorite. Before you do that, we need to tell you something important that can influence the outcome of this assessment.

BE HONEST.

When we take these types of tests, we tend to answer projecting who we would like to be, but not who we really are. The MBTI is designed to assess our NATURAL tendencies. You might currently be in a job or environment, like Theater Arts, that forces you to be an extrovert in many areas. Given your natural preference, however, you would rather not talk to many people. So, when asked to agree or disagree with a statement like: "You find it difficult to introduce yourself to other people." the actor in you might tend to disagree, but outside of theater, you would agree. In that scenario, you would want to answer based on how you actually feel in normal situations, rather than what you have learned to be comfortable with because of a job, club or sport.

Make sense?

There are no right or wrong answers. The test takes twelve minutes for fast readers and twenty minutes for slow readers, like me. Try not to mark anything neutral, unless you feel strongly about being neutral. Once the test is complete, read about your personality type and record it, along with it's strengths and weaknesses about your type in the area here.

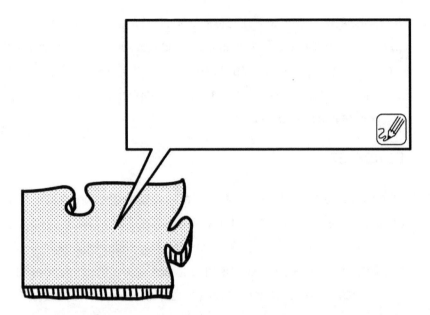

Most students we have worked with over the years have felt this test has greatly helped them become more self-aware. Occasionally, we run into someone who will take the test and feel it is way off. If that is you, we would strongly recommend you go grab a close friend or relative and retake the test with them at your side. Sometimes having someone who knows you well to answer with you can help.

Remember, shortcutting any of these steps is only going to hurt the level of clarity and direction you receive from this book. Investing in yourself like this is not easy and takes time, but we promise it will lead you down the path you want to go.

You are doing great so far!

PUZZLE PIECE #7 Love Languages

If you are a dude, your first goal is to not get weirded out by the title of this chapter. Here is the truth - if this were the only chapter you took seriously in the entire book, you will learn enough about yourself and others to make a radical difference in the world. Here is another truth - if you have any desire to ever be a good father or husband you will need to be equipped in this area.

Dr. Gary Chapman does a brilliant job of helping us wrap our minds around five basic expressions of love, aka, love languages. Each of these you will see expressed by God in Scripture and in the leaders that God raised up. It's one of the final, key unique factors that make you, you. The five love languages, as noted by Dr. Chapman's work are:

Words of Affirmation

Acts of Service

Receiving Gifts

Quality Time

Physical Touch

While we are each capable of expressing all of these, sort of like spiritual gifts, we tend to lean on a few of them as our 'go to' expressions of love. A key point in Dr. Chapman's work here is that we tend to express love the same way we desire to receive it. For example, my top love language is receiving gifts. I love buying gifts for others and find it frustrating when someone hands me a gift that they did not put much thought into. On the flip-side, I hate to be hugged. Physical touch is not my cup of tea so I tend to shy away from patting people on the back, holding hands, or any other form of contact.

Normally, being weak in this love language area of physical touch is not a problem, at least until I run into someone who greatly values it like my daughter Aliza. It's in situations like this that knowing my love language becomes so key. When Aliza is in most need of comfort from her dad, she might appreciate an act of service such as me cleaning her room for her, but it is a thousand times more meaningful to her if I give her the biggest hug and kiss I am capable of. When I do, it's me learning to go against my natural love language of giving gifts to speak her love language of physical touch which fills her tank up more than anything.

Imagine you were running an orphanage somewhere in the world and your goal was to build these precious children up in the way God created them. Wouldn't it be important to be able to recognize each child's love language and make sure you are communicating God's love in a way that can best receive it?

This sort of love language insight can help you draw the best out of others. It can help you lead and motivate. It can help you comfort those who are hurting. It can also help you communicate to others how they can best express love to you when you need it the most. Love languages are the native tongue of healthy relationships and it is very difficult to do anything meaningful in this life without developing strong relationships with those around you.

Paul himself was a champion of love languages. Although he never used that term specifically, he did go into detail in many of his letters about how exactly to love the world around us. In this passage, he uses the phrase "share their burdens". This was an early church expression for having empathy and helping others when they are in great need. Sometimes it would mean they would provide words of affirmation, sometimes it would be an act of service. It was clear Paul wanted the Galatian church here to consider who they were uniquely made to be and us that to love and impact others.

Live creatively, friends. If someone falls into sin, forgivingly restore him, saving your critical comments for yourself. You might be needing forgiveness before the day's out. Stoop down and reach out to those who are oppressed. Share their burdens, and so complete Christ's law. If you think you are too good for that, you are badly deceived. Make a careful exploration of who you are and the work you have been given, and then sink yourself into that. Don't be impressed with yourself. Don't compare yourself with others. Each of you must take responsibility for doing the creative best you can with your own life.
Galatians 6:1-5 (MSG)

Well said Paul. A careful exploration of who we are is something that most people on earth will never take time to do. Not the case with you though! Let's take a few more minutes to flush out what your top love languages are as we prepare to put all of these pieces together.

Action: Go to www.5lovelanguages.com and take the test or do an online search for 'free teen love language test'. It should take about ten to fifteen minutes max. When finished, record your top two love languages here and something you learned about them.

CHAPTER 14

PUTTING IT ALL TOGETHER

O kay, now it's time to zoom back out and take a look at the big picture again. We did this exercise in the last section but now we want to include a few more pieces and take another look. If this seems redundant and you find yourself tempted to skip this, don't. We were very intentional when we laid out the flow of this book. One of the biggest obstacles to discovering purpose and busting through the barrier of normal is impatience. Self awareness evolves as we methodically take time to analyze ourselves and is not something that can be microwaved.

Let's add our personality type and love languages to the mix and follow our three step process one more time.

Action

Step 1: Fill out your answers from the previous chapters (6-9, 12 and 13) and look for connections.

Take note of what you read about your personality type, specifically its strengths and weaknesses. Do you see any connections between the strengths of your personality type and the passions you have? Same goes for your love language. Can the way you like to show and receive love help you live out some of your passions?

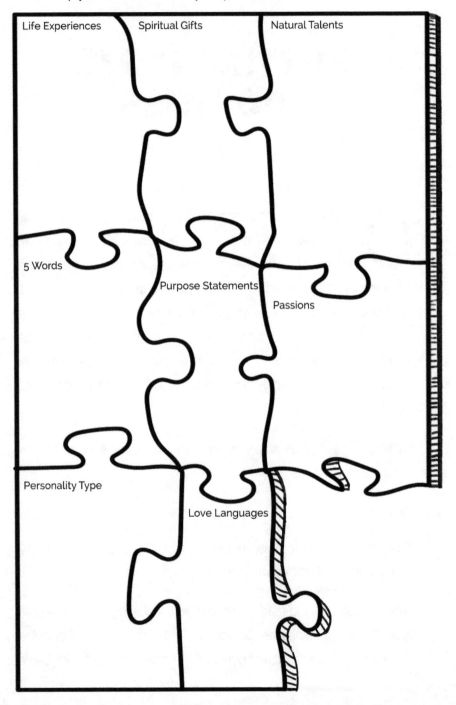

Step 2: Draw a line between connections you see and look for themes.

Remember that a theme is like a main idea. Did adding in your personality type and love language help affirm a theme you saw before or reveal a new one you missed? Maybe both?

Step 3: Connect your themes to your passions with a purpose statement.

Consider this your second draft at attempting to write a purpose statement now that you added two more pieces to the puzzle.

"I can see myself doing _____ for _____, because I would be excited to see _____."

If you come up with a another purpose statement, that is great, but it's not a problem if you don't. If you still feel stuck, remember you have a few options.

1. Show five people your puzzle overview from this chapter and ask for their input on what themes they see and what purpose statements it might result in.

2. Consider taking advantage of a thirty-minute or one-hour coaching session with our team. We will look at what you have written down so far, ask you a bunch of questions and help you think through possible purpose statements. To learn more about our coaching sessions, go to www.throatpunchnormal.com.

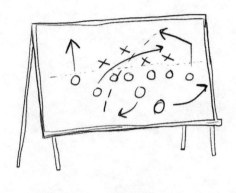

SECTION 4

YOUR STRATEGY

Congrats! You have made it to the toughest section of the entire book, but you are about to ace it. If you love strategy games, this is going to be a cakewalk. If strategy games drive you nuts, it's not because you are not capable of developing or understanding strategy, you just don't enjoy the mental exercise as much as others do. There is nothing wrong with that.

The goal of Section Four is to help you narrow down your focus into a mission that God has created you to excel in. We will go a little deeper on your strengths and weaknesses, help you find support to get started, and empower you to begin bringing your unique purposes to life.

CHAPTER 15

PUZZLE PIECE #8 PURPOSE STATEMENTS

With all of this freedom God has given us to use our talents to impact the world, it can be overwhelming to try and pick a direction. It's common to feel torn with competing passions knowing you can't do it all. Focus helps you narrow down on one path at a time so that you can do it really well. Depending on how time consuming some of your passions are, you might be able to pursue more than one at the same time.

It's now time to finalize a purpose statement to pursue. If you are still afraid of making a 'wrong' choice, then it's probably a good time to remind you that the only wrong choice is not choosing any of them. There are tons of purpose statements you could actually make because God has put a very diverse set of unique talents, life experiences, passions, etc., within you.

It is possible to start down a path only to later find out that you might not be as equipped as you thought you were. Maybe you over estimated your talent and find yourself struggling with something you thought would be easier. I used to be able to crush a baseball when I played with my friends after school. So I was very surprised to find myself striking out during Little League games against pitchers who knew how to throw curves and fastballs. I would eventually decide to drop baseball and pick up soccer, which I was a little better at.

Sometimes we are just afraid of wasting time, money, and energy on something that may not work out. And that's normal. Trying anything new is a risk and our natural inclination is to avoid risk. But here's the problem:

You will never find success without risk.

Risk is just part of the equation. Risk leads to failure and if you want to do something with your life that is meaningful, then you need to learn to embrace failure. Risk and Failure are your friends. Risk and Failure are here to toughen you up. This world needs people who can overcome their fears of failing and push forward anyway. That is what it means to be courageous.

Let's acknowledge our fears as being real because they will not really ever go away. They can however, be managed and even help us develop courage, which is absolutely needed in order to bring our dreams into reality.

Action: It's best to have at least two, but no more than five purpose statements. The following exercise will help you narrow this down to one. Write each statement in the box provided, and in the column to the right, add a tally mark for each statement that meets the following criteria:

Purpose Statement	Score

- Add 1 mark if the statement is in line with something somewhat aligned to what you are already doing in life or at school
- Add 1 mark to the statement you get most excited about
- Add 1 mark to the statement that lines up with something you are already good at
- Add 1 mark to the statement that best fits your Myers Briggs Personality Type. If you are not sure, google career options for your personality type, e.g., "ENFP Careers"
- Add 1 mark to the statement that you think has the highest probability of becoming reality
- Add 1 mark to the statement that a friend thinks you should pursue

- Add 1 mark to the statement that most closely connects to a very impacting life experience that you have had
- Add 1 mark to the statement that you most likely have the time and resources to pursue now
- Add 1 mark to the statement that you think will draw out the best in you if you pursue it
- Add 1 mark to the statement that would make the most impact in the lives of others
- Add 1 mark to the statement that you feel you would gain the most support for from others if you pursued it
- Add 2 marks to the statement that you will most regret never going after
- Add 2 marks to the statement you would be willing to sacrifice the most in order to see it happen

Out of a total possible score of fifteen, which purpose statement came out on top?

In the event of a tie, go with the one that you will most regret never going after, or that you would be willing to sacrifice the most for. When we punch out of this life, we will all have regrets. Now is the time to decide which regrets you can live with and which ones you can't. If you pursue something and it does not work out, at least you will never have to live with the regret of not trying.

To me, never trying is much worse than trying and coming up short. It's is extremely rare to hit a home run with your first attempt at something, but the more at-bats you give yourself, the higher the chances you have of eventually knocking one out of the park.

Chosen your purpose statement? Let's record it here.

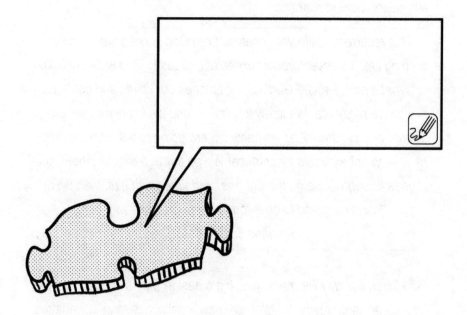

Starting something new is always exciting. Expect your motivation to come and go as the level of adversity you encounter increases, but this is all part of the journey. You got this.

If you have any doubt about whether your purpose statement is any good or is even something you can do, go ahead and punch that line of thinking in the throat too. You are making the most educated guesses any human can make at this point, when it comes to purpose and direction. You have already learned so much about how to self-evaluate that even if you stopped right here, you would probably have more self awareness than most people in their thirties do.

But you are not stopping....this is only the beginning. With your chosen purpose statement in hand, we are going to dive deeper into the idea that you were created to take risks. Take some time to reflect on Paul's affirmation here in Romans.

This resurrection life you received from God is not a timid, grave-tending life. It's adventurously expectant, greeting God with a childlike "What's next, Papa?" God's Spirit touches our spirits and confirms who we really are. We know who he is, and we know who we are: Father and children. And we know we are going to get what's coming to us—an unbelievable inheritance! We go through exactly what Christ goes through. If we go through the hard times with him, then we're certainly going to go through the good times with him!
Romans 8:15-17 (MSG)

God loves the way He made you. It's a design that is specific, unique, intentional, and ready to take on new challenges and adventures. Getting started is always the hardest part, but God left plenty of hacks on how to do it. So let's get ready to move from ideas to actions as you embrace the purposes you were made for.

STRATEGIC GOALS AND ACTIONS

"Setting goals is the first step in turning the invisible into the visible."
– Tony Robbins

Creating Short Term Goals and Strategic Actions Around Your Purpose Statement

If you have arrived at this part of the book before solidifying your purpose statement, you are moving too fast. Being impatient in this process will come back to haunt you at some point.

Let's assume you are ready to go. What exactly do you do next? How do you know you are taking the right steps down this narrow path?

The answer: It begins with creating a short-term vision.

Your short-term vision is something that you can realistically accomplish within the next three months to three years. It's looking forward, but not so far forward that you lose stamina during the pursuit.

The elements that make up your short-term vision statement include the following:

1. Practical milestones you need to achieve in pursuit of your chosen purpose statement.

2. Something that will require discipline, sacrifice, and focus.

Short-term vision statements are fluid. They can change as you learn from your experiences and pursue new passions and opportunities.

Here is an example of mine.

> Chosen Purpose Statement: I can see myself <u>starting a 24-7 teen center</u> for <u>all teens</u>, because I would be excited to see <u>them have access to people who care about who they are and where they are going personally, professionally, and spiritually</u>.
>
> Short Term Vision: To establish our first 24-7 teen center with diverse and sustainable funding sources.
>
> ✓ It is something that can be done within three years.
>
> ✓ It includes milestones. (Securing our first location and having the funding to maintain it.)
>
> ✓ It will require my discipline, sacrifice, and focus.

Your turn. In the space below, write out your short-term vision statement.

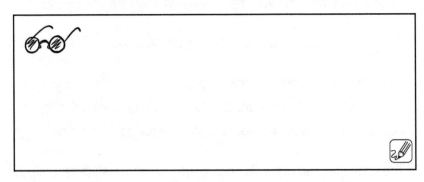

Around this short-term vision, we will now create some goals and strategic actions. These will become your focal point over the next twelve weeks and will be updated when the period is over.

Why twelve weeks?

We want to build and keep momentum. How many times have you set a New Year's resolution, only to give up on it in February? Annual goals are good, but quarterly goals create a sense of urgency to get things done. From now on, we encourage you to goal-set in twelve week increments. Try it for at least three months before you make a decision, in order to see whether or not it works for you.

Focus on Three Strategic Actions

In light of your short-term vision, what are the three most important things you need to accomplish first and can do so within twelve weeks?

Using my purpose and vision statements above, here would be an example of mine:

1. Research and interview five teen center directors somewhere in my state and ask them how they got started.

2. Research how to write a business plan and find a mentor who can help me write one.

3. Begin to build a team by sharing my vision with twenty people I think would be interested in helping.

HINT: They should be specific and measurable. Here are some more examples...

- Find five people that can help me achieve my goals and ask for their help
- Invite six of my friends to church and don't give up until at least two actually come
- Volunteer at a shelter for ten hours to learn about homeless ministry
- Watch three hours of tutorial videos online

Now it's your turn. List what you think your top three strategic actions are. Once this is done, you are ready to launch! Well...almost. There is one last piece to discuss. Plans always look pretty on paper, but without accountability and a team around you to help, the odds that you will get very far are low. Nothing great is ever accomplished alone.

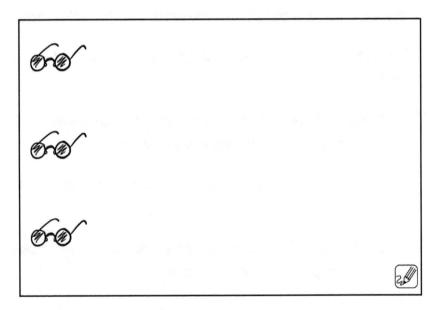

CHAPTER 17

PUZZLE PIECE #9
BUILDING YOUR
TEAM

I f you just kept reading without actually DOING anything from the last chapter then you need to read this chapter twice. Having the right people to hold you accountable to what you say you are going to do is game changer.

Let's consider what Paul's team would have looked like as the early church was being formed. You may have heard about Timothy, Paul's young apprentice and partner in ministry to whom he wrote a few letters, but what about everyone else that made Paul's mission possible? In order for the apostle to successfully navigate through the religious turmoil in the first century he needed some folks he could rely on. Read any of his letters and you will find no shortage of credit given to dozens of people who provided him shelter, work, food, wise counsel, and encouragement. They helped him write letters, collect and deliver offerings between churches, provide pastoral care, and continue educating Christians when he was not around.

The entire sixteenth chapter of Romans is one long list of people Paul is thanking and sending shout outs too!

The good news is that for now, you don't need a team as large as Paul's. Instead, let's focus on finding five solid people who can help challenge you, counsel you, and draw out the best in you.

Here is what you are looking for: This Fab Five must be...
- ✓ Knowledgeable
- ✓ Supportive
- ✓ Able to tell you the hard truth

Their knowledge base should be diverse. In other words, if your focus is to be an influential leader on your soccer team, don't just grab five soccer players.

Let's use my short-term vision statement as an example: "To establish our first 24-7 center with diverse and sustainable funding sources."

If I was just getting started down this path, and it was literally day one, I already said my top three strategic goals would be:
- Market Research - Talk to those who have established teen centers in the past
- Creating a Business Plan - Envision how ours will be set apart and function
- Find Strategic Partners - Network to find others who share my passion

With these three goals, I would be looking for mentors who, respectively:
- Have run a non-profit for teens and would be willing to support my efforts
- Have created and executed business plans in the past and can give me guidance

- Are interested in sharing in this work with me as volunteers, board members, or partners

As someone who wants to be more of an influential leader on your soccer team, you might look for people who are:

- Already doing a good job leading their respective teams or clubs
- Coaching teams and understand what it takes to lead others
- Great mentors because they listen well and care for others even better

Maybe you are already thinking of one or two people who would be great, but five?! That's a stretch.

Don't worry, most of us would struggle here. This is why we are going to challenge you to do something we rarely see teens do.

Network.

Personally, I hate networking. As an INTJ personality type, my preference is to not interact with humans at all. However, I also know that the things I am passionate about have no chance of happening if I don't push myself out of my comfort zone daily. Networking is one of many ways I must do that.

The best place to start networking for people that can provide great support to you and your mission is social media. Start with people that are closer to you, message them about what you are doing and how you specifically need their support.

When I did market research on "teen centers," there were none in my area, and the people I knew didn't know anyone I could connect with in that field, so I went to Google. I found teen centers across the USA, picked up the phone, and starting talking to any of the founders or directors I could.

I learned so much doing this. None of these people ended up being a permanent part of my team, but that's ok. When I shared my vision with people in my church, several came forward and wanted to get involved. Many even became my first board members.

As your goals change, so should some of the people you surround yourself with. Keep looking for people who can speak wisely into the areas you are focused on.

As part of your Fab Five, you should also be looking for:
- ✓ Someone who shares your passion in this area.
- ✓ Someone who will support and encourage you no matter what.

These are your special advisors. They are in the loop regarding what you are doing. They can help you find resources, cheer you on, have your back in prayer, and be your listening ear.

Now here is something you need to remember: Putting a great team around you takes time. Make it your goal to develop your team within the first twelve weeks, but don't get frustrated if it doesn't happen. Be patient. Share your vision for the road ahead with others, and you will eventually cross paths with the people you want around you. Some hang around for months – and others years.

When you have identified your five, the ask is simple. Tell them what you are doing – your goals – and think of one thing they can each help you with. It will be on you to schedule times to connect with each member of your team and determine how often you talk. Here are some examples of the roles you might be looking to fill:

- Accountability - Meet for coffee or lunch once a month to talk about how things are going – your wins and failures.
- Prayer - Keep someone in the loop who is praying over your mission.
- Administrative Help - If your mission is way bigger than you, think about the types of help you might need and who would be great at running your events, marketing, handling money, etc.
- Training - Can you find someone who has already done what you want to do? Ask them to train you or coach you through the process.
- Mafia Man - Find the person that always seems to have connections or hook-ups for everything. Someone this well connected is your Mafia Man. When you can't find the help you need, they can.
- Cheerleader - Everyone needs that one person around them that is always positive. No matter how bad things get, having a cheerleader in your corner that is great at encouragement will help you through the days when you want to give up.

Consider this your own personal board of directors. When people know what you want to achieve and how they can specifically help you do it, they are more likely to commit to supporting you. Never quit trying to put the right people around you, and be quick to remove those that derail your momentum. Your team is your own personal eco-system. It's an environment designed to bring your unique purpose to life, so develop and maintain it well.

For each role you list, write down the names of at least two people who could fill that position on your team. You only need one person to say yes to each spot.

Thinking part is over. Now go make this plan come alive by making some calls. If you are panicking right now because you don't know what to say, here is a sample script but you need to make this fit your personality:

Hi _____!

I don't know how to make this not sound weird. I respect and value your opinion as a leader and as someone who knows how to bring out the best in others. I'm being challenged by a book called Throat Punch Normal *which is helping me understand my unique design and how I can make an impact in the world around me.*

At this point, my current goal is to really use my influence as an athlete to be a better leader and get to know others on my team by serving, listening, and encouraging. My hope is that my faith in God will shine through my actions and lead to more meaningful conversations with my teammates.

I know I'm going to fail some and even feel like quitting at times so I need someone in my corner to encourage me to keep going when that happens. Would you be willing to connect with me once a month as a source of encouragement and support as I focus on this goal?

Sincerely,

Lebron James

There you have it. Go make this wording your own, resist the temptation to take action alone, and get ready to do some damage. If you want, with the last puzzle piece added, you can copy all of your other pieces and have one complete picture to look at. You are the only person in the world with this mix of pieces. Pretty cool, huh?

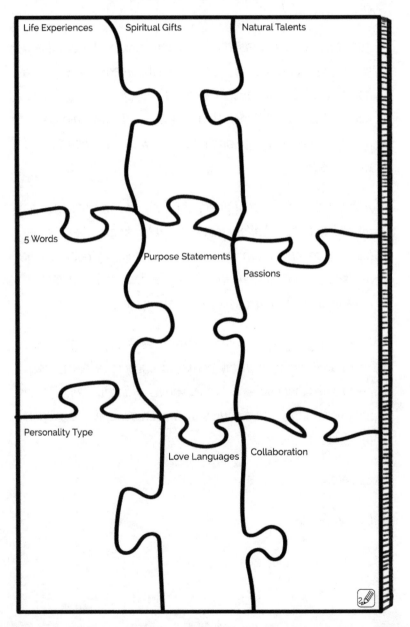

CHAPTER 18

YOUR PERSONAL
SWOT ANALYSIS

WARNING: This section puts your self awareness to the TEST!

will be short and sweet, because this analysis might take a little more time. But, I promise it will be worth it!

"If you know the enemy and know yourself, you need not fear the result of a hundred battles."

That quote is from an old, old book called the *Art of War*. The truth inside of it led the powerful Chinese army to success and now drives many of the most powerful businesses in the world.

These businesses have taken this truth and created a tool that puts it into action. The SWOT analysis helps take a look at ourselves and what's happening around us, in light of our chosen focus or purpose, by dividing things into four quadrants:

Strengths - What specific strengths are going to help you live out your purpose statement?

Weaknesses - What specific weaknesses will make it difficult to do so?

Opportunities - What things, outside of yourself, will help you achieve your strategic actions?

Threats - What things may hold you back?

Strengths and Weaknesses are both things that are internal (from within you) while Opportunities and Threats are external (from the community around you).

Example of Strengths

- What skills, certifications, education, connections, or experiences give you an advantage?
- What do you do better than others around you?
- What comes easy to you?
- What do other people (parents, peers, etc.) see as your strengths?
- What is an achievement you are proud of?
- What do you value in yourself, but may not see when you look at those around you?

Examples of Weaknesses

- What do you avoid because you don't feel confident or don't like doing it?
- What will the people around you see as your weaknesses?

- Where do you not have education or training?
- What are the common weaknesses associated with your personality type?

Example of Opportunities

- What new tech can help you? Paul didn't have apps or YouTube?
- What teams, groups, mentors or friends around you can help you? Can you talk to someone who is doing what you want to do?
- Is there a need in your school or the world that no one is filling?
- Is there something your friends complain about often?
- Are there events, classes, or opportunities around you?
- Can you gain experience now? What are areas around you where you can test the waters now?

Example of Threats

- What obstacles do you currently face at school or at home?
- Could any of your weaknesses lead to threats?
- Are there people or situations around you that take you away from your purpose or bring you down?

Paul's SWOT Analysis

If Paul were to fill out a personal SWOT analysis it might look like this...

-Education - VISION
(given a thorough
Jewish education)

-Strategic Reasoning
(understood audience)

-The gifts of
the spirit

-understood
culture and
pagan mythologes

-Great communicator
(unconventional, but
wise teaching)

-had experience as
a Pharisee and had
much power

-Holy Spirit
filled
miracles
+ devotion

-content with
weaknesses,
insults, hardships,
persecutions, and
calamities

-Thorns in the flesh-
Some guess Paul's thorn
could be a temptation, a
chronic eye problem, malaria,
migraines, epilepsy, or a speech
disability

- natural
tendencies

S W
O T

-Story/shared
background

-The way things had
always been done

-Had support
of others in
early church

-False
Gospels

- Self glory

-"messenger of
Satan"

-Ship wrecks

-had encouragement
of friends (Barabas)

-Alexander
the coppersmith

-The people
he was
reaching

Action: Using the guidance and example we have provided, go ahead and complete your own SWOT analysis.

There it is, your map to success all out on paper.

Hopefully through these tools you learned a little bit more about Paul and a lot more about yourself! Most businesses will review their SWOT analysis once a year or anytime they come upon a landmark decision. This is good practice for our personal lives also. The self awareness you have practiced here will not only help you create a guide for these next few chapters but will also help you punch normal square in the throat.

CHAPTER 19

PLAYING TO YOUR STRENGTHS

With your personal SWOT analysis complete, we can now zoom in a little closer on your strengths. This is a great time to revisit your strategic goals and actions from Chapter 16 to make sure they align with the things you are really good at. To do this, you must look at each strength you listed and ask yourself this question:

How are my strengths going to help me achieve my goals?

As an example, let's say your goal is to start a new club on campus to raise awareness about depression, suicide, and various kinds of mental health issues that impact teens. Your SWOT lists these areas as your strengths: detail oriented, administrative, artistic/creative, compassionate, and hardworking.

Looking at your strategic goals you know that in order to launch the club you need a teacher to sponsor it, club officers, and members who get excited about the purpose and vision. You may not be the most persuasive speaker and being an introvert, you don't really know a ton of people that you feel comfortable inviting to be a part of your club, so where do you begin?

The artsy/creative side of you is raising it's hand. You decide to leverage your strength here by creating a series of eye-catching, inspiring posters and flyers to place around school that direct people to a social media page you created which talks about the club's mission and vision with photos, videos, blogs and more. Since you are strong administratively, you have already written out officer roles and job descriptions for the club so that when your peers begin following your social media site, you can begin sharing with them ways that they can get further involved.

The focus here is learning how to map your strategic actions back to your strengths. Using this same example, let's say that one of the opportunities you have in your SWOT is that a very famous actor and singer has just come forward with their lifelong struggle with depression. It's on TMZ, it's in your SnapChat feed, people are talking about it, and you recognize that the topic you are so passionate about is on everyone's mind. So the question you ask yourself is:

How are my strengths going to help me take advantage of this opportunity?

You leverage your creativity once again to build awareness for your new club by purchasing a t-shirt with a picture of the embattled celebrity on it and using neon ink you write "Depression is Real" as large as possible on the back. You wear that shirt to school every day for a week and each student that comes up to you asking what your shirt is about is a student you are promoting your new club to. Sure, it's embarrassing being a walking billboard all week but your compassion for those suffering from mental illness pushes you through.

When you learn to make a habit of taking action based on your strengths, you will win more than you lose. There are times when you will have to operate in your weakness and may need to get up in front of people to talk when you would rather write a letter and have someone read it but as long as you didn't set out to become motivational speaker, WHO CARES that you suck at public speaking!

Should you try to improve on your weaknesses? Sure! It's just not a big priority. Your strategic goals and actions are your priority and if you don't use your strengths to focus on those, you may never get the opportunity to stand up in front of a crowd in the first place.

If you find yourself at a place where many of your action items are things that you are not very good at, then delegate as much as possible. Part of delegating is asking others who are strong where you are weak for help. This ties right back into the importance of having a strong team around you before you take action. As amazing and as brilliant as you are in some areas, you will always accomplish more with a diverse set of talented people around you.

Don't obsess over your weaknesses. Acknowledge them, plan around them, and zero in on your strengths. Master this skill and success will be waiting for you on the other side.

Action: Take some time to analyze each of your strengths in light of your strategic goals and actions and the opportunities that are before you. In the space provided, detail your ideas on how your strengths can help you achieve your specific goals and take advantage of specific opportunities.

CHAPTER 20

LEARN BY DOING

"For the things we have to learn before we can do them,
we learn by doing them."
– Aristotle

Sometimes life needs you to read the manual, but most of the time it just needs you to get in the car and drive. New things can be scary at first. A fear of failure lurks over some more than others and life can feel like one big science experiment. You create an educated hypothesis about something, but then you must conduct the experiment. If it doesn't work, you adjust and try again.

This is exactly what this book is preparing you to do - pick a course of action based on a deeper understanding of how you are made, jump in with both feet, step back and evaluate, make adjustments, and do it again. This is your winning formula in life. You don't have to stress about getting it all right, because you won't. You just need to be willing to learn from what didn't go according to plan and adjust before you go at it again.

At this point, you have positioned yourself in a great place to chase after what is most meaningful to you. Now it is time to commit to putting ideas into actions, with both feet!

You have more focus and direction now than most people ever have in their entire life. A thousand people may purchase this very book, but the clear majority won't even make it past Section Two before quitting. If you got this far, I know you love learning. In order to be a true catalyst however, you must love *doing* just as much.

It's way easier to talk about doing stuff than it is to actually do it. Fear of failure is our enemy's most reliable weapon. If you want to avoid being taken out by it, then you have no choice but to keep going until you finish this book.

Take a moment to look at what you have equipped yourself with so far:
- ✓ A deeper understanding of the strengths and weaknesses of your generation
- ✓ A unique map of who God made you to be
- ✓ Growing confidence in the fact that you do have a calling that is both general and specific
- ✓ A focused purpose and short term vision of the future
- ✓ A team around you ready to help you succeed
- ✓ A strategic next steps action plan

And, in these upcoming sections:
- ✓ A blueprint of how the enemy will try to take you out
- ✓ A knowledge of the most important components that will determine your success

You have the makings of someone who is ready to take the fight to the enemy!

The more you put all you've learned into action, the more battle tested you become. You will not only be leading yourself well, but leading those around you as they watch. Everyone has some degree of influence, but yours is about to hit another level. Commit to being an action oriented person, with a "nothing-to-lose attitude," and you will look back on a life that was lived to its fullest.

As we turn to the final sections, be encouraged that your diligence through each activity in this book will pay off. Jesus' brother, James, would likely agree.

Don't fool yourself into thinking that you are a listener when you are anything but, letting the Word go in one ear and out the other. Act on what you hear! Those who hear and don't act are like those who glance in the mirror, walk away, and two minutes later have no idea who they are, what they look like. But whoever catches a glimpse of the revealed counsel of God—the free life!—even out of the corner of his eye, and sticks with it, is no distracted scatterbrain but a man or woman of action. That person will find delight and affirmation in the action.
James 1:23-25 (MSG)

Action: We challenge you to warm up your 'taking action' muscles. List three simple things (related to anything in your life) you know you need to stop talking about doing and just do them.

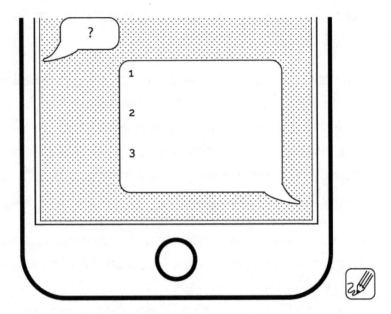

Now choose one and go do it before you continue reading another page of this book.

SECTION 5

YOUR ENEMY

There are times in life when all your worst nightmares of what can go wrong are confirmed. It was halftime at my daughter's middle school soccer game and as the coach, I was losing my cool. We were down 0-2 and getting out hustled. Every time a ball was kicked toward one of our players they went ducking, flinching and cowering like they were about to get hit by a grenade. So at halftime, I decided to hold up a soccer ball to my face and scold them for being scared of a piece of rubber filled with air.

"What's the worst thing that can happen, girls?" I shouted. "You get nailed in the face with the ball. It stings. You shake it off and move on!"

During the opening play of the second half, our center forward took a direct shot to the nose and blood began gushing everywhere. Worst nightmare confirmed. Both teams took a knee in horror as the blood just couldn't seem to stop. She was immediately rushed off the field and the game resumed.

Ten minutes later, the team was in shock once again as their center forward came walking back to the bench with her entire jersey and shorts stained in dry blood. Without hesitation, she re-entered the match and I watched in amazement as the level of courage and resolve of the team soared to a whole new level. With only minutes left, she would go on to score the game tying goal.

In Section Five, things will get very real and at times, very dark. We are, after all, at war. Your enemy could not care less about your plans to make an impact on the world or be like Jesus, because he has too many weapons as his disposal to derail you. You only become a threat when you learn to take a ball to the face at close distance, get back up, and do it all over again. That kind of resolve is in you and our hope is to help you unleash it.

CHAPTER 21

THIS DECEPTION IS THE GOAT

GOAT. It's a sports term that stands for "Greatest Of All Time."

Deception. As a teen, you are well familiar with this concept. Don't get offended, it's not a shot at your character. The art of bending the truth is something we all learned to do right about the time we decided to walk. As toddlers we realized that often the louder we scream the faster we get attention. By the time we hit Pre-K, we learned to leverage this skill to get our annoying siblings in trouble, play sick to avoid school (but not too sick to provoke a doctor visit), or play dumb when getting interrogated about the latest broken object around the house.

We like deception. It just sometimes makes life easier – and easy is our default love language. I mean, sure, it's not as much fun when you find yourself on the receiving end of such duplicity, but it feels like it works for us more than it does against us, right?

Let's consider for a moment what could be the greatest deception of all time when it comes to students your age.

Could it be the deception that you are young and have plenty of time to get your life straight? That's a good one because we know that tomorrow is no guarantee.

Could it be the deception that you are a victim of bad stuff happening to you (divorce, abuse, bullying, depression, neglect)? That one feels like truth because everyone alive has been the victim of some type of injustice at some point; however, the deception of perpetually feeling like a victim is one that keeps most in bondage for life, and prevents us from living boldly.

Maybe the greatest deception over every teen is the theology that all paths lead to God? Whatever you believe about Jesus, God...it's all good because we will all probably end up in the same place. No need to tell people about Jesus or engage in any sort of 'evangelism' if this is the case.

Man, there are so many good ones to choose from, aren't there?

What if the "GOAT" regarding deceptions, impacting teens all around the world, is simply this:

Nobody cares.

Nobody cares what you think. Nobody cares what you do. Nobody cares about anything or anyone but themselves.

We know this isn't 100% true, but it sure feels like it is most the time.

Think about how many times a day you think or say the phrase "I don't care." This is a self-preservation phrase. We say it to protect ourselves from failure, disappointment, embarrassment, and anything we deem as a threat to our often fragile self-image. Sometimes we use it harmlessly because we truly do not have a strong opinion on what we eat or watch, etc., but there are way too many times we evoke this language to escape a difficult situation, conversation, or decision. Escape is easy. And remember, we love us some easy.

Ultimately, the problem with the deception of not caring and believing nobody else does either is that it's a trap designed to suck you dry of the very being God uniquely created you to be.

Ever done any gardening? Before you can plant anything you must dig the hole and clear it of weeds and anything that might prevent growth. Deception is like the mother of all weeds. As a teen, you have thirteen to nineteen year's worth of these things filling the hole, so how can you expect to fully embrace your unique design until you get some things cleared out?

Identifying deceptions is the first step. Surrounding yourself with truth comes next. But for now, your goal is simply to identify.

The thing that has me so upset is that I care about you so much—
this is the passion of God burning inside me! I promised your hand
in marriage to Christ, presented you as a pure virgin to her husband.
And now I'm afraid that exactly as the Snake seduced Eve with
his smooth patter, you are being lured away from the
simple purity of your love for Christ.
2 Corinthians 11:1-3 (MSG)

This is not just Paul's heart for the Christians in his time, this is God's heart for YOU today! The virgin/husband stuff may seem a little weird to you but what you need to remember is that your specific design transcends life here on Earth. Every piece of you—your life experiences, natural talents, spiritual gifts, personality type, passions, and more—was designed to be a beautiful reflection of God for eternity. God cares deeply about the decisions you make on a daily basis, INCLUDING the decision to believe thoughts about your identity, purpose, and belonging that are just not true.

A healthy and accurate self image is vital to live a life of meaning, purpose, and impact. When our focus drifts from Christ, so does everything else. We will talk more about how to stay focused on what matters most in a little bit.

For now, let's focus on the topic at hand and dig up some weeds before we begin planting.

Action: Take a moment to consider the adverse effects of deception in your life. Maybe it's that you never feel "good enough" for _____. Is there a negative thought you continue to have about your looks, your body, your personality? I know we are diving into more heavy stuff here, but it's important. List what you believe might be the three greatest deceptions (lies) that might be impacting you this year and talk to someone on your collaboration team about them. Dragging these false thoughts out into the open is a throat punch that lands on your enemy every time.

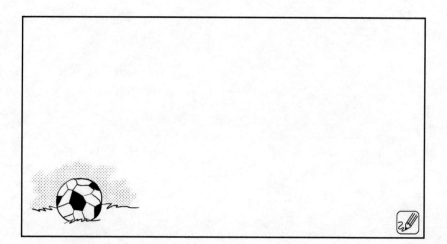

JOE ELLIOTT

CHAPTER 22

THE DAYS ARE EVIL

"Make the most out of every opportunity because the days are evil."
– Paul to the Church in Ephesus

I f you made it this far, I believe it's because at the end of the day, you want to live a life that truly matters. You have demonstrated that you are willing to learn, willing to be challenged and ready to put this all into practice. What you need to know now is that all of Hell is focused on making sure that all of this great analyzing and planning amounts to nothing.

Why?

Because we are at war.

Pain, suffering, despair, violence, etc. surround us and even creation can sense that something is not right. When we hear about a mass shooting, political scandal, terrorist attack, racial profiling incident, and more, our level of grief over these evils has been reduced to five second social media posts as our desensitized hearts move on. When the regular occurrences of these types of injustices cease to motivate us to any sort of action, evil is winning.

Mankind is no stranger to these types of evils. During the first century, when the Apostle Paul saw the depravity within the church at Ephesus, he made a point to remind those early Christians that they were in a war.

God is strong, and he wants you strong. So take everything the Master has set out for you, well-made weapons of the best materials. And put them to use so you will be able to stand up to everything the Devil throws your way. This is no afternoon athletic contest that we'll walk away from and forget about in a couple of hours. This is for keeps, a life-or-death fight to the finish against the Devil and all his angels. Be prepared. You're up against far more than you can handle on your own. Take all the help you can get, every weapon God has issued, so that when it's all over but the shouting you'll still be on your feet. Truth, righteousness, peace, faith, and salvation are more than words. Learn how to apply them. You'll need them throughout your life. God's Word is an indispensable weapon. In the same way, prayer is essential in this ongoing warfare. Pray hard and long. Pray for your brothers and sisters. Keep your eyes open. Keep each other's spirits up so that no one falls behind or drops out.
Ephesians 6:10-20 (MSG)

As is the case for any war, it is imperative that we know our enemy. Whenever we set out to do something "good", we find ourselves battling an enemy that loves to attack our body and mind. This very book has been like boot camp. Not everyone makes it through boot camp, but those that do are ready to take the fight to the next level.

In a world that is hungry for hope, your quest to embrace and refine who God made you to be matters more today than in any other point in history. We would be doing you a disservice by not talking about all the ways you have been, and will be, attacked. To take advantage of the opportunity this life has provided, you must strive to be a person of influence each and every day. Here is a look at five weapons our enemy uses to take us out of the battle. As you read through them, consider the impact some of these might be having in your life today.

Doubt

It's the oldest trick in the book, literally. The devil questioned Eve's reasoning in the garden and planted a seed of doubt about whether she understood God's words correctly. Doubt continues to plague all humans and infiltrates every aspect of life. We doubt our intellect, our relationships, our appearance, our faith, our self-worth, our talent....on and on.

Doubt will stop you from applying anything that you learn in this book. To overcome doubt, you must lean on the ancient definition of faith found in Hebrews 11:1.

"Faith is confidence in what we hope for and assurance about what we do not see."

Your confidence and assurance DOES NOT come from everything working out exactly as you hope. That will rarely, if ever, happen. Your confidence and assurance comes from knowing that God desires to help you commit to developing your gifts and passions and never quit. Ultimately, your success lies in your ability to keeping moving forward DESPITE YOUR DOUBTS over and over again.

Endurance

If Hell can't get you with doubt, it will aim for your stamina, banking on the hope that there will only be so much adversity you can take before you quit. To battle against this, you must always have the end in mind.

Let me give an example.

After completing the very same exercises you just did in the previous sections, I realized my passion was to help others find theirs. I set very specific goals about who I wanted to help, how and where, but this was not the end I had in mind. My end is not even physical in nature, it's spiritual. My goal is to be more like Jesus by the end than I was in the beginning of my life.

Every day I wake up and face a new set of challenges preventing me from doing this. And, if I allow myself to become discouraged in the present, I take my eyes off the future. The only way I fail is by quitting.

So, if everything I desire to 'do' in this life falls apart, I will be disappointed, yes. However, I will have in my possession the one thing that cannot be taken from me - my choice to be more like Jesus. Having an end in mind like this helps you handle the disappointments that are bound to come along the way. You will lose battles but you can still win the war if your mind is focused in the right place.

Environment

A very popular podcast I listen to, "Entrepreneurs on Fire," ends every episode with an encouraging challenge. The host, John Lee Dumas, tells his listeners that they are the average of the three to five people they spend the most time around. We see this truth play out in many aspects of society, and it's largely true. You are who you hang around as we mentioned in Chapter Three.

If you desire to take all your talent and see it thrive, you must plant it around others who will water it. Surrounding yourself in a nurturing environment will not happen overnight. You will need to be patient; you will need to network and develop new contacts; and you will need to try things you have never tried before. This is why we dedicated an entire chapter to the concept of collaboration and building a team. If you kinda skipped through that part because you felt the team thing was a little overkill, it's not too late to go back and spend some time developing this part of your strategy.

Or do what Hell is whispering in your ear to do - which is doubt you will ever find a better environment to plant yourself in and give up trying.

Past Failures

Yep, you've got plenty of them. We all do! If I were your enemy, I would love nothing more than to get you stuck reliving your past mistakes. Any time you attempt something new, I would be right there to remind you that you will fail again, just like you did last time... maybe even worse.

Overcoming this trap is easier said than done.

Mistakes are vital to future success. They are our greatest teacher. They invoke emotion in us and that emotion is a powerful motivator. For some, when reflecting on past mistakes, the emotion of fear rises to the surface. For others, determination flares up. One of these emotions works against you, the other for you.

The key to choosing which emotion you embrace when past failures resurface is in knowing that God foreknew all your screw-ups and that knowledge did not, even for a second, make Him hesitate in His choice to give His Son to die for you.

God uses your past failures to bring humility into your life. Humility is a powerful weapon against an enemy consumed by pride. With humility, you can glance into the past and give thanks to God that you not only survived these failures, but you grew in character as a result.

Hopelessness

It is reported that one in five people suffer from depression. As a leader who has coached people of all ages for some time now, I see that hope is being robbed from our world. The thief is brutal and loves to see us destroyed.

God came into this world as the embodiment of hope through Jesus. To remove hope from our equation is to remove God from the center of our purpose - the ultimate win for an enemy who is only at war with humanity because he cannot win against God.

Faith is being sure of what we hope for. Faith makes everything you are about to embark on possible. Without faith, there is no hope. Without hope, humanity will lose this war.

One Final Thought

I hate to lose! The very thought of an enemy that is out to steal, kill, and destroy pisses me off. It invokes in me a desire to go to war, punch evil in the throat and sacrifice whatever is required to destroy it.

This emotion was not always alive in me. It was cultivated by putting myself in positions to see the impact of evil up close. If you find yourself in a place where you are more numbed than stirred by the depravity in this world, I would encourage you to draw closer to the pain that others are suffering.

Maybe that means spending time with a homeless person in your city to hear their story. Maybe that is saving up money to go serve on a short mission trip. It could mean attending some local non-profits' event to hear why they are passionate about their cause.

Life is too short to not be all in. Your goal in completing this book is to get your bearings on where you have been and where you are going. Once you pick a direction, commit to being all in. This world is so desperate for you to make the most of every opportunity because the days are, in fact, evil.

Action: Take some time to consider areas that might take you out. If you can think of anything that has ever stopped you from doing something in the past, write it down here. Refer back to the threats you wrote down in your SWOT analysis, too.

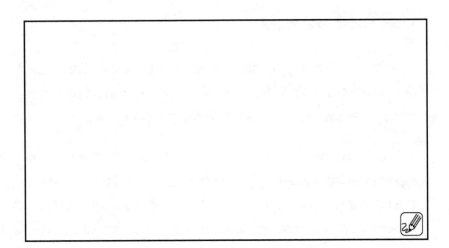

CHAPTER 23

A LETTER FROM THE OTHER SIDE

In the 1940s C.S. Lewis wrote a series of fiction letters that was unlike any other Christian work ever written. The letters were written from Hell's point of view and were addressed from one senior demon (Screwtape) to his nephew, a junior tempter (named Wormwood) so as to advise him on methods of securing the damnation of a British man, known only as "the Patient".

Reading this book messed me up in a good way.

What if, for a few minutes, God pulled back the invisible curtain and exposed you to Hell's specific plans to steal, kill, and destroy your life? Would what you see and hear change the way you live and think?

That's what reading C.S. Lewis' book, *The Screwtape Letters*, did for me.

I'd like to modernize this idea by sharing a letter with you from Hell's vantage point and ask that you pretend you are a 'junior tempter' (demon) who is receiving this counsel on how to prevent teenagers from impacting their campuses. Imagine you are attending a lecture at a university with thousands of other demons packed in there with you.

Each of you is assigned specific teens that you are to prevent from becoming self-aware and using their gifts and passions against you. Words like subject, patient, client will all refer to humans. When I say 'the enemy' I am referring to God and when I say 'Lord or Master', I am referring to Satan.

I know some of you may be uncomfortable with this but I tell you, there is no safer place to peer behind the gates of Hell than in the company of the Holy Spirit. It would be unwise in any war not to study the enemy's tactics, so let's flip the script for a moment and ask God to bring us revelation as we take a look at this spiritual battle in the heavenly realms.

_____

Very warm greetings my fellow tempter,

This letter is intended to give you a brief introduction into "How to Trap a Young Human." I will cover 3 steps in crafting reliable traps and conclude with some general advice at the end. I understand you are new to this war so I will make my advice to you as direct and clear as possible.

Realize that humans have a natural rebellion within them that they primarily aim at our enemy so they really do most the work for us. However, our end goal is not distraction but destruction! So we are going to focus on some of the basic philosophies behind planning and setting traps for your humans. There are thousands of effective ways to trap these pathetic creatures but for today we only intend to give you an overview. Let's begin.

First Things First – Plan and Prepare

Before setting the trap, think ahead. Consider the type of human, the stage of life they are in, cultural influences, family upbringing, past pains and hurts, etc. This is all very important in customizing your traps.

Since all of your subjects live in sector twelve, also known as America, many of them will attend a church. This is not a great concern as most of our finest traps have been laid in and around churches. In general, you will typically find the young American subject to be hungry for acceptance, identity, and purpose, envying their friends, living to please themselves with little self discipline and having a deep fear of being perceived as "unaccepting".

So you can begin to see what I mean when I tell you they have already done half the work for us!

Start by examining their past. Where do their fears and past hurts lie? Were they sexually abused as children? If so, perhaps they have a lower self confidence that can be used against them? Have they been abandoned by a mother or father? Perhaps there is some unforgiveness there we can use to lure them further into darkness?

Maybe they had very few hardships in their childhood and received much of what their hearts desired. Great! This means they may have expectant, entitled attitudes and since they never had to really work hard and sacrifice for anything in their earlier years they will not have the stamina to fight against the onslaught of our temptations.

Is your subject lonely? Depressed? Angry? Insecure about who they are or how they look? All of this plays into the permanent traps you will design for them. Study your human carefully and envision their demise before you begin.

WARNING: There are great potential risks involved in trapping humans as many of your colleagues have been far too ambitious in their methods and inadvertently drawn their subjects toward our enemy. The pain they suffer while trapped should be very light and gradual to begin with. It has been proven that traps that are too traumatic for humans can often bring them to a point of desperation in which they will only seek advice and listen to the enemy. We must keep them in darkness, whatever it takes.

After you have studied your subject, come up with a contingency plan. What happens if the pain, trials, and hardships your humans endure while trapped actually draw them closer to our enemy? What if the human is more resilient than you first believed? We know that the source of their power comes from the authority they were given from heaven so your contingency plan should focus on cutting off the source of that power by distracting them from prayer and meditation on our enemy's words.

Need I remind you that should both your traps and contingencies fail, we will have a young human on our hands capable of causing much damage to sectors of our dominion.

Second, Gain Their Trust

Set the stage before setting the trap. Scatter samples of the bait throughout their life; if humans can enjoy an appetizer, they'll be more likely to enter the trap for the main course. Here are some great examples of effective bait for our young patients:

Mobile devices and social media accounts - Feed their envy and insecurity! Show them the relationships they wish they were in, the hangouts they wish they got invited to, the talents their friends have and they don't. Keep them obsessed with self image and addicted to needing attention and approval

Relationships at home - the more division the better. Keep their parents busy, their siblings irritated.

Procrastination - Help them feel like there's no rush. The more they put off, the more they get behind in school and at home. This increases their stress and young people do not handle adversity of any kind well, so it will lead to self mutilation, depression, and all kinds of wonderful traps that can keep them in bondage for decades.

Video Games and Entertainment - use this to fill them with a false sense of productivity and purpose.

For some it is a good idea to give them a taste of worldly success, expose them to the praises of men, reward them with popularity, and let them marvel at their accomplishments. When they seek to take a break from the daily grind of school, introduce them to chemical addictions if possible. It is a common belief in this American culture that anything in moderation, as long as it doesn't hurt anyone, is permissible. Alcohol, nicotine and marijuana are great appetizers because even if it's only for a short time, they are not thinking about anything else but escaping, pleasing themselves, relaxing because they 'deserve a break'. This is exactly the kind of mindset we want to promote in our patients. Over time it grows into a dependency as they develop more of an appetite to escape reality by any means necessary.

While I am on the subject, let me warn you. If your human finds himself growing dissatisfied with their normal means of escape then you must find a new appetizer to gain their trust and do it quickly. Otherwise, they will begin to contemplate meaning, purpose, our enemy and that leads down a very dangerous path for us.

Now in order to gain their trust for the long haul, your patients must be willing to compromise and be led more by their emotions than by truth. Once the traps become their idol, and by that I mean the object of their affection that they worship above our enemy, you have them right where you want them! From here on out, the focus becomes more about maintaining the trap and finding them small pleasures in life to snack on. It used to be much more difficult for us than it is today to find such meaningless pleasures that keep them distracted but now most humans even carry around non-stop sources of entertainment in their pockets from childhood so the possibilities are now endless. We have affectionately been referring to these devices as Hell phones.

The point is, if you can't find something to get your human addicted to you're just not trying.

Gain their trust! Remember, your bait should cause little ill effects short term. Our pornography empire, currently worth over twenty billion, began with the simple deception that humans were not in fact created in the image of our enemy nor were their bodies living temples. Purity is overrated and impossible to live out. Simple deceptions such as these bait humans down a path of destruction rather quickly. As you studied in your "History of Destruction" course, bondages to pornography have given birth to one our fastest growing empires: Child Sex Slavery.

Human slavery is our second most lucrative endeavor behind the illegal sale of weapons.

Finally, Set the Trap

Remember, our enemy loves to turn our traps against us and the things we mean for human harm, he uses to bring freedom into their lives. So in picking a trap, make sure it lines up with the weaknesses that exist within them.

A young patient's desire to fit in or be accepted is where we want you to start – they will go to great lengths to find a group that will accept them. Become that group for them! Bind them to other students with similar interests and hobbies as theirs but make sure there is absolutely no light in the others you are yoking them to. The last thing we need is the infectious diseases of truth and revelation spreading through their campuses. Those are plagues that we have spent decades exterminating. Pretty soon even the slight utterance of our enemy's name will bring young people so much persecution that they will not dare bring him up in order to maintain their approval from friends. It all boils down to this for the young ones, being liked.

So let's win their heart through music, movies, celebrities, and more. Let's glamorize our ways in their sight, show them how much of a buzz-kill serving our enemy is.

I would highly recommend encouraging your young subjects to date as early as possible. Dating is a very reliable trap. It fulfills their hunger to be noticed and loved and also sets them up for great pain and heartbreak later on. You will notice that young humans have very little self control when it comes to sexual temptation. If you enslave them to these desires when they are young, you will trap them for life.

You must understand, our father deploys most of our resources against the younger humans because the payoff is so great. They are naive, driven by emotion, ruled by impulse, selfish, prideful, easily deceived, believe all the propaganda we feed them, lovers of rebellion, and when other light-filled humans try to warn them of our traps – they don't listen to their advice. We are beginning to see that our traps are so effective with the young ones that over time it has robbed them of the disgusting qualities of holy ambition and courage.

In our present age, they are so used to living in bondage that they don't even mind it or even feel they are trapped in the first place. This, my fellow underling, is exactly what we have been striving for.

Another common weakness that leads to a reliable trap is a young patient's desire to retreat. When life gets hard, weak humans retreat. When they do retreat, make sure they have someone to blame as well. This allows them to hold on to their meaningless dignity while they abandon their enemy-given leadership roles. If you can get the church attending ones to leave their church that is best, but if not, there are other baits that are just as effective.

They can be physically in the church community but not mentally or spiritually. Keep them passive. Can you imagine what would happen if we were dealing with a culture of young humans who really knew who our enemy created them to be? What if they really knew what they were capable of through our enemy? Very scary thought. The bottom line is that their natural inclination to retreat is a very reliable trap, use it daily.

By the way, there is a balance to all of these traps. Don't lure your subject to a point of such dissatisfaction in life that they begin seeking purpose and meaning. I have already warned you about this but should you become so zealous in squeezing the joy out of your subjects it will backfire on you. Instead, find them small pleasures that keep them going day to day. Small pleasures such as food, entertainment, parties, sex, games, and more, give humans things to look forward to in the middle of their mundane routines. As long as they keep chasing those pleasures over and over again they will never develop a hunger for our enemy.

I'd like to conclude with some general tips and advice for trapping humans.

Deny them a sense of urgency – one of my favorite words in the English language is the word 'later'. Have you noticed that humans are always going to start doing things 'later'? THEY WILL GET TO IT LATER, THEY WILL THINK ABOUT IT LATER, THEY WILL TALK ABOUT IT LATER. Now is never a good time for them, it's always inconvenient, they always have reasons and excuses for doing something later. There is no sense of urgency and that is how it must remain. Our enemy urges them to make every moment count so we must be proactive at urging them that those moments don't have to start now, they can start later!

Keep them busy – The more time you have them focused on trivial work the better. Jobs, sports, school, and other activities must fill their lives. Leave them little time to reflect on anything eternal. AND MONITOR THEIR TIME IN PRAYER AND MEDITATION ON TRUTH!!!

Rule their thoughts, dominate their emotions – <u>every demon knows that truth is really what we are at war against</u>. So rule their thoughts by keeping truth out and dominate their emotions by baiting them to act on impulse and not reason. Woo their heart. Appeal to their mind and you have them.

Let them go to church, give to the poor, donate their money, etc. as all these things bring a false sense of fulfilled purpose to their lives. Let them go through the religious motions, just don't let them become transformed in the likeness of our enemy's son. This will destroy us all!

There have been periods of mass transformations in certain quadrants throughout history. Revivals, as humans like to put it. While these are extremely destructive to our lord's empire, we are thankful these things are always short lived. If you find yourself dealing with a human that is going through one of these personal revivals or awakenings, the best thing to do is cut your losses for the moment and return back when their passion and enthusiasm for our enemy simmers down as it almost always does.

Finally, and need I remind you of this, don't ever quit! Most humans don't believe this sort of warfare even exists, but even the ones that do often grow weary of fighting us. Our lord does not quit and neither do we. There are always weaknesses in humans so find them. Exploit them. Bait them. Trap them. Demolish any significant dreams, hopes and ambitions they have that stand in the way of our owning their purpose and effectiveness here on earth.

May death, destruction, and darkness rule in all of your regions.

Action: When we read about Satan and demons in the Bible, we see that there is, in fact, strategy. This chapter can be a lot to take in but the simple goal is to get you thinking about where you are vulnerable. What if you really did have a demon assigned to you? Would knowing that change how you lived in any way? What types of bait would he be laying out for you right now?

This is a great time to pause and pray. Pray for wisdom and insight. No matter how you feel about the role spiritual warfare may play in your life, ask God to reveal to you truth. Consider doing your own research on this topic in the Bible. The more you shed light on this, the less space you give the enemy to hide in.

CHAPTER 24

THE ART OF TAKING A THROAT PUNCH

As the last few chapters have highlighted, your path to bringing your unique purpose to life will not come without great challenge. Your mind, your heart, your resolve will all be tested over and over again. Have you ever spoken up in class to give an answer to a question only to be super embarrassed by a teacher who mocks your response in front of everyone? It has happened to all of us at times and when it does, what do we tell ourselves? Fear and anger flare up and we vow to never answer another question in that class again.

Over something as simple as a moment of embarrassment, we quit. If, as humans, we can be this easily derailed, it's no wonder that most of us never live up to our potential.

Adversity will come in waves and take many different forms. Sometimes circumstances are out of your control but it's not so much about what happens to you as it is how you respond to things happening. How you react when life punches you in the throat matters.

The Domino Effect of Character Building

Let's think about your response to the first punch you take like it's the first domino in a set that is ready to be tipped over and begin a chain reaction. That punch can come in the form of fear, embarrassment, doubt, heartbreak, failure, or a thousand other hindrances. To follow our example earlier, you just decided that your mission this semester is to become a more vocal leader in the classroom. That first time you speak up, all your worst fears are confirmed as the teacher and entire class laugh at what they deem as a very idiotic statement. The punch has landed, the first domino is tipped and sets off the next one in the chain, which is fear. Fear then knocks into doubt because you wonder if anyone will ever take your leadership seriously again. Doubt bumps into withdrawal who lands on top of sadness who then hits surrender. At this point you have to decide whether you want to set the dominos all back up again or just quit playing altogether.

OR here is the other scenario to consider,,,

You try something and fail (get punched). That failure knocks over into doubt but this time you have set the dominos up differently. Because you were expecting to get hit with doubt, doubt tips over into both withdrawal AND resolve, setting off two different reactions going on within you simultaneously. One path represents the way you feel, the other path what you do. While you emotionally still feel the sting of fear, doubt, withdrawal, sadness, and surrender shooting through your veins, you decide to follow the other path triggered by resolve. Resolve connects with hope, hope pushes into belief, belief taps courage and courage allows you to get back up and either take another punch or deliver one back.

Anyone can learn to get back up a few times after taking a punch, but learning to do it over and over again takes great patience. Almost more than anything else, the Apostle Paul wanted the early church to develop patience in their hardships. Here is a snippet from his letter in Romans:

We continue to shout our praise even when we're hemmed in with troubles, because we know how troubles can develop passionate patience in us, and how that patience in turn forges the tempered steel of virtue, keeping us alert for whatever God will do next.
Romans 5:3-4

It's no secret that God desires to develop our character while evil is out to destroy it before it ever has a chance to take root. Humans can never experience growth without also being willing to experience failure. The good news is that you are already a pro at failure!

Let's look at some of the things you have failed at thus far in life.
- ✓ You have lied to people.
- ✓ You have talked trash about people behind their back.
- ✓ You have taken things that do not belong to you.
- ✓ You have been insensitive at times.
- ✓ You have used words to tear people down rather than build them up.
- ✓ You have implemented ideas that didn't work out.
- ✓ You have made a judgement about someone and been wrong.
- ✓ You have quit on things too soon.
- ✓ You have let people around you down.

And this is just the warm up. You can keep going for another few pages if you feel inspired to. You have screwed up a ton!

And yet, you are still here, alive, seeking to make the most out of this life you have been given.

Despite your epic fails, you still have hope. And hope keeps you moving forward even when the reality of failure looms. That's right. Failure in some form is imminent yet again in your life and if I were you, I would learn to embrace it. Humility cannot exist without failure and humility is the secret ingredient to developing Godly character and navigating through this rollercoaster of life.

Here is a checklist of what failure does for the resolve of the humble.
- ✓ Protects us from arrogance
- ✓ Tests our faith
- ✓ Brings to light areas where we are weak
- ✓ Builds our character
- ✓ Exposes our fear
- ✓ Inspires honest evaluation
- ✓ Teaches patience
- ✓ Advances wisdom
- ✓ Strengthens our strategy

Failure is life's most proficient teacher. Its lessons are painful, but the absence of its education would be far more damaging. Failure is the best friend you always wanted but never had. It is here to ultimately remind you once again that success in this life is not about what you are doing but who you are becoming.

This world is longing for young, courageous men and women who are not afraid to fail. Failure is an event, not a medical condition. There are a number of epic fails still scheduled for your life and no matter how conservatively you live, you won't be able to avoid them.

Your best course of action is to let failure do what it was designed to do - toughen you up for the war you find yourself in. There is no room for victim mentalities on this journey. Bad stuff happens to good people all the time; you are not immune to it. You will either make the most out of what you have to work with or spend the rest of your life being sad and angry about what could have been.

The choice is yours.

Action: Embrace adversity by choosing to be thankful for the things it's intending to produce in you. If you forget what those are, read through the list in this chapter again. Now add to the list by taking time to list out the positive things that your past failures have drawn out of you.

CHAPTER 25

STAYING FOCUSED AND MOTIVATED

Your ability to stay focused and motivated on this journey is the fire you need to kindle. We want to highlight some ideas that we think will help. However, this is something you have to continue to experiment with over time. Reflect on times in your life when you have been the most motivated and make a note on why you think that was the case.

Here are a few tips...

Study Your Motivational Patterns

The list of motivators that exists in life is extensive. The book, *What Motivates Me*, by Adrian Gostick and Chester Elton, is one of many great resources you can find on this topic. Understanding your motivational patterns should be part of your learning goals at some point.

To give you an idea of what you are trying to look for, here are a few common motivators people have:

- Money
- Recognition
- Impacting Others
- Problem Solving
- Autonomy (doing stuff on your own)
- Achievement

If you are motivated by impacting others, for example, you should measure your progress not by money or recognition, but by the stories you encounter of people you have helped. Everyone is motivated by something. When you pinpoint yours, make sure you think through how to create some goals around these motivators.

Inspiration Wall

An inspiration wall is literally a wall in your room that inspires you to stay focused on your goals. Not everyone can afford to designate an entire wall to something like this but at least a desk area or shelf is better than nothing.

On my inspiration wall, I have movie posters the symbolize the level of risk and sacrifice it takes to bring something you are truly passionate about to life. I also have memorabilia in the form of pictures and letters from lives impacted. I encountered a homeless man in California selling his homeless signs to pedestrians walking by. I was so impressed with his creativity that I bought his cardboard sign for twenty dollars and placed it above my desk to remind me of the power of innovation.

When you design your inspiration space, it should remind you of the big picture in life. It should highlight victories, cultivate hope, and draw out the warrior within you. Try it. Send us a picture when you're done, too. We would love to be inspired with you.

Journal

I'm kind of bad at this, but I can tell you that pulling out my journal and reading the few entries that do exist is motivating to me. On a personal note, my journal has helped me to see the evidence that God is, in fact, real. I have recorded dreams that have become reality and words that were spoken to me by strangers who didn't know me but were dead accurate. I even documented some of my deepest prayers and have seen many answered.

Documenting the journey will help you remember that the sacrifice is worth it. You can push through your current afflictions because you have before. Circumstances always change over time and a journal can be the perfect testament to that.

You don't have to journal every day. Start by doing it once a month for a year. If it helps, awesome. If not, at least you will have some amazing archives of your life waiting to be discovered by your future grandchildren when you check out.

Calculate Regret

I have a go-to question I ask myself every time motivation is running low. If I stop doing what I'm doing right now, will I regret not persevering through later in life?

If my answer is yes, I let the fear of regret motivate me forward.

We can't go back, only forward. So, we all must make choices today about how we want to live tomorrow. As we said earlier in this book, we will all acquire some level of regret. My goal, however, is to not accumulated any more of it than necessary.

Action: Use the area on the next page to think about times in your life that you have felt most motivated and why. Do you see any consistent themes? What do you think your top three motivators are?

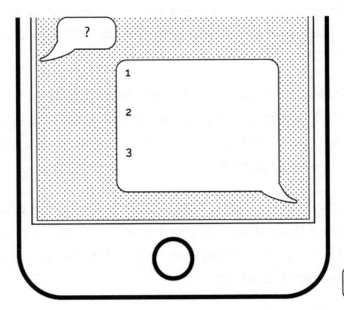

YOUR PERSPECTIVE

O ur thoughts dictate our actions. All the seemingly insignificant things that race through our mind every day are actually either pushing us toward or pulling us away from something. If you have made it to this final section and you are filled with more doubt than confidence in your ability to go put your plans in action, the enemy has you pinned. It's not an impossible grip to get free from but you will have to make a stand against your fears and doubts at some point in order to break loose.

We hope that some of the truth in these final chapters will help set you on a path of freedom as you embrace your uniqueness and live out the purposes God created you for. At the very least, this will set your mind on what matters most, what your true identity is, and what you can do to just enjoy the ride.

CHAPTER 26

IT'S NOT ABOUT YOU

U p until this point we have talked a lot about aligning our gifts and talents with our potential passions, but here is the curveball. It doesn't always work out like you want it to. Sometimes we are led to go down a path we would rather not go.

Remember the story of Jonah? This was the guy who got swallowed by an enormous fish because he decided to run from an assignment God had for him. He wanted nothing to do with speaking to the Ninevites.

Remember how much Moses tried to convince God he was not the right fit for the job? It's true. One of the most famous biblical leaders of all time tried to convince God that he should go find someone else to do the job.

Both of these guys knew exactly what was being asked of them but had zero desire to do it. Paul had plenty of experience with this as well but he learned early on that pain is part of the process of embracing purpose...

But there is another urgency before me now. I feel compelled to go to Jerusalem. I'm completely in the dark about what will happen when I get there. I do know that it won't be any picnic, for the Holy Spirit has let me know repeatedly and clearly that there are hard times and

imprisonment ahead. But that matters little.
What matters most to me is to finish what God started.
Acts 20:22-24 (MSG)

It's true. Although we have been given freedom to use our God-given gifts to fight this spiritual war, we still have a commander and He still selects us for assignments we would rather have nothing to do with.

In 2008, God nudged me to lead what would turn out to be one of the most successful ministries I never wanted to be a part of. You read that right. The 6th St Prayer Team was my calling and my nemesis for years. It was also the scene of the most bizarre thing that has ever happened to me in ministry.

And it all began because I asked God to use me to make an impact in Austin, TX. Let me explain how this went down.

At the time, I was the youth and college pastor at a growing church in the city. The Bible studies were great but I knew we needed to do something more. For several months our college group had prayed about what we could do to serve our city. We found ourselves praying often for a section of Austin called 6th St. To imagine a typical weekend night you have to picture a Mardi Gras parade with thousands of people packed into a downtown city street with tons of bars, live music, street acts, homeless people, drunk pedestrians, patches of vomit here and there, officers and police barricades at every corner - it's the ultimate block party times a hundred. Anything can happen down there and it so often does.

So you can imagine the confused look on everyone's faces when I suggested we remove our prayers from our cozy house gathering and take them to the streets at night, right in the middle of the madness. Some loved the idea, others felt we would just be setting ourselves up for failure. I knew this idea was not of my own because as soon as I mentioned it, I was already silently praying that everyone would say no. Unfortunately, twelve brave, young warriors said yes, so I had no choice but to be all in.

Our first night prayerwalking 6th St was fairly uneventful. We would stop every few blocks and huddle to pray. When those walking around us took notice of what we were doing, they would laugh, take pictures and blurt out the occasional sarcastic remark or obscenity. Praying publicly in these environments is like take a golf club to a hornets nest. You can do some serious damage to the nest but not without getting stung.

After an hour of prayerwalking, we decided to call it a night and head back to our cars. That's when it happened. The most bizarre interaction I have ever had with the Holy Spirit and another human.

Just in front of us we saw a younger looking man dressed head to toe in black. As we drew closer, the smell of vomit and beer became like a freight train barreling through our senses. What looked like a mask from a block away turned out to be tattoos covering his entire face, throat, and body. Piercing and chains were everywhere and in his hand was a whip. As we approached, we could hear him mutter the words "I'll whip you for five dollars." It was a very generous offer but our group walked around him without stopping, like he was Moses parting the Red Sea.

Fortunately, we all made it past him alive. That, however, is when the Holy Spirit nudged me to go back. After a brief, three second inner dialogue where I told God what I thought about that idea in very raw form, I decided to obey. So without a plan or clue as to what I was going to say I just blurted out the first thing that came to mind as I approached: "Hey man, I tell you what, how about I give you five dollars if you let me pray for you."

There was a brief moment of silence as he considered my offer followed by him taking a few steps closer to me as he leaned into my personal space and asked me if I had been drinking. That's right, the homeless looking guy who smelled like a sewer wanted to know if I was drunk! I suppose my offer was not one he came across very often so I assured him I was completely sober.

With assurance that I was in my right mind he proceeded to drop his whip, take of his hat and hold his arms out like a cross and said "Ya, f*** it. Go for it" as he bowed his head and closed his eyes.

At this point I turned to wave down the rest of my group desperately trying to get their attention. A few noticed what was happening and the group came running back to assist. Without hesitation, we circled around and began praying. About one minute into the prayer, it happened. To everyone's surprise, the man dropped to his knees and began crying. I'm not talking a few sniffles here, I mean the ugly kind of crying that you don't think grown men are capable of. This sparked a new level of intensity in our prayers.

After the dust began to settle and prayers came to a close, the man slowly stood up and began to tell us his story. His name was Arson. He had been traveling around the country for some time, just wandering. No real direction or purpose. He slept on the street some nights, or would crash with others if he could afford it. He told us he used to be a Christian. There was a church he loved in California but he was hurt by many of the people whom he thought were his brothers and sisters in Christ. That's when doubt crept in followed by a series of unfortunate events that developed in Arson a bitterness toward God.

That bitterness turned to hate and hurt that sent him in the downward spiral we found him in.

He removed his shirt revealing even more tattoos. There were some bible verses, an upside down crucifix and that marking around his neck - that was the hand of Satan representing the grip he knew the devil had on him. Looking at him was like reading a journal of the turmoil he had encountered in life archived all over his body. He sincerely thanked us for stopping and praying for him stating that he honestly didn't think Christians like us still existed. It had been so long since he had encountered anyone brave enough to overcome his appearance and speak to his heart.

We really didn't know what to do at that point so we offered to take him out to eat with us. He quickly turned it down and said "Look, if you really want to do something for me, bring me to church."

Again, not the reaction we were expecting!

We did end up bringing Arson to church with us the next day as we witnessed the healing process begin. He came back to church by catching a local bus from downtown the following week. Then he came again, and again, and again.

Most Christians will go their entire lives without ever seeing a transformation as radical as this. A year after first encountering Arson on 6th St, he would leave Austin and take his newly restored relationship with Jesus with him as he began his own ministry reaching those on the streets like him - the ones everyone else wants nothing to do with.

As far as our little ministry experiment went, after that encounter, we knew we had to go back. The 6th Street Prayer Team came to life that summer and is now celebrating it's 10 year anniversary as a ministry. Having prayed for thousands of individuals over the years, seeing miracles first hand and lives that have been impacted, we could fill an entire book with stories like Arson's. It was by far, the most successful ministry I never wanted to be a part of.

Sometimes, despite our careful calculations of how we think our gifts and passions align, God calls us to toss that to the side and just follow Him. This life is not about us.

So as we draw near to the end of our time together, we want to encourage you to pay careful attention to what God may be whispering to you. Expect Him to pitch the curve so when it comes, you are ready to knock it out of the park.

CHAPTER 27

TRUE IDENTITY

Athletic careers end, friends move off, and we still get pissed off at the people around us. Maybe you are a proud Texan, a republican or democrat, or in your first real relationship. You can be acing your AP class, or just trying to get by. You might be on top of the world because of something a friend said, or down and out because of different words from that very same friend.

All of these things will fight to be your primary identity but they're not. There is a more true version of you out there. Close your eyes: can you see it?

It is the version that God carved out before the formation of time itself and it is always calling to you, pushing you forward.

By focusing on this truth we can live lives anchored and not be tossed by the waves! Take a quick glance at some of the words God uses to describe you and me.

- *Accepted*, Ephesians 1:6
- *Loved*, Ephesians 1:4
- *Adopted*, Ephesians 1:5, 6
- *Forgiven*, Ephesians 1:7
- *A child of God*, Romans 8:16
- *A friend of Jesus*, John 15:14

- *Saved by grace*, Ephesians 2:8
- *Chosen*, John 15:16
- *Complete*, Colossians 2:10
- *Redeemed*, Galatians 3:13
- *Rescued*, Colossians 1:13
- *Cared for*, 1 Peter 5:7

- *Blessed*, Ephesians 1:3
- *Healed*, 1 Peter 2:24
- *Eternal*, 1 John 5:11, 12
- *A new person*, 2 Corinthians 5:17
- *A masterpiece*, Ephesians 2:10
- *An heir*, Romans 8:17
- *A temple*, 1 Peter 2:5
- *An example*, Ephesians 5:1
- *Declared not guilty*, Romans 3:24
- *Not condemned*, Romans 8:1
- *Made right with God*, 2 Corinthians 5:21
- *Led by the Spirit*, Romans 8:14
- *Living by faith*, 2 Corinthians 5:7
- *Being transformed*, Romans 12:1, 2
- *Not afraid*, 2 Timothy 1:7
- *Strong in the Lord*, Ephesians 6:10
- *Victorious*, Romans 8:37
- *An overcomer*, 1 John 4:4
- *A co-worker with God*, 1 Cor. 3:9
- *A workman*, Philippians 2:13
- *One in Christ with other believers*, Galatians 3:28
- *Part of the Church*, Eph. 5:29, 30

The Christian life is all about replacing our trials, feelings, and doubts with what is most true about us.

Action: Out of all the things God says about you, which stand out to you the most? Write down three and then take the top verse and hang it somewhere that you will see it often.

CHAPTER 28

THE GREATEST RESCUE MISSION OF ALL TIME

Ask anyone who knows me and they will tell you, I'm a sucker for a good underdog story!

Greatly outnumbered, their back against the wall. Three hundred soldiers lock shields and brace for the incoming attack. (I am inspired to do at least thirty sit-ups)

Up against the ropes in the final round, the nobody from Philly charges the champ (ROCKY, ROCKY, ROCKY...I air box and throw my hands in victory)

Back from the dead Neo steps into his Identity, and the bullets slow to a halt in front of him (I KNOW KUNG FU)

A sacrifice against insurmountable odds, these are the stories worth telling.

I'm convinced that all of the best stories echo with themes of the gospel. The small pieces that they share are enough to compel us to more but even the best stories we tell pale in comparison to the one written 2000 years ago.

God in all his power and love, steps into the human story in the form of a humble baby. He takes on our appearance, our struggles, and our pain. The God of the Bible is not a far off God removed from your situation or your searching but instead freely choses to get involved.

He grew up a man, an underdog born to refugees in a manger. Jesus went to school, ate, slept, and grew daily. He put up with siblings, parents and indigestion (crazy human frustration), all for the sake of us. And as He steps into the human story He changes our story forever.

As a man He traveled giving His life to teaching and guiding others, restoring sight, homes, and hearts to Him. He traveled with a rag tag team of twelve and miracles followed them everywhere they went. He was a super-hero in its truest form...but yet He continually faced rejection.

Just like in all the great moments from all the greatest films, Jesus found Himself in a place where this story could head one of two ways. And in that moment in a small garden, kneeled in prayer, Jesus chose the path God laid out for Him and turned Himself over to the very traitors that He Himself had created. He was beaten, broken, and finally laid down His life to complete the greatest rescue mission of all time. In the faultless life, brutal death, and glorious resurrection of Jesus, God saves humanity from itself. We no longer have to carry the weight of all our mistakes, Jesus offers to carry them for us. In Him we see a new future for humanity and if we choose, His life and power can now be our life and power.

"God put the wrong on him who never did anything wrong, so we could be put right with God."
2 Corinthians 5:21 (MSG)

What if I told you the story wasn't over! In fact, for those who make the decision to choose to follow Jesus, the story is just beginning.

"I tell you the truth, anyone who believes in me will do the same works I have done, and even greater works, because I am going to be with the Father."
John 14:12 (NLT)

You are now royalty in a kingdom unseen, the Kingdom of God, and as royalty, have divine duties laid out before you.

You are a part of the rescue mission.

Our duty is not only to harness the potential of our unique design and make the best of it, but to reflect the image of our Creator and Savior, the perfect man Jesus.

We are faced with this question: How will we live in this new kingdom? Will we choose our own right/wrong and lookout for ourselves or choose God's right/wrong and use our gifts for others?

We can now follow in Jesus' footsteps spreading seeds of peace, patience, and love, restoring those around us to the God of hope!

Through Jesus' example we move the human project forward!

God has given us the task of telling everyone what He is doing. We're Christ's representatives. God uses us to persuade men and women to drop their differences and enter into God's work of making things right between them. We're speaking for Christ Himself now: become friends with God; He's already a friend with you.

If that's too hippy dippity for you, let me put it simply: Jesus is not physically here but you and I are. It is through believers and the church that this world hears the good news. So if you see something that breaks your heart, pray on it and act. God uses you to be a part of the answer.

The gifts, passions, and hardwiring you have so patiently uncovered in this book serve as tools in the hands of God as He uses you to level roads of injustice and invite God's people back into relationship with Him.

A lot of times we have the idea that saving the world is the job of the pastor or at least someone else. However, that couldn't be further from the truth.

All the gifts of the Spirit and the same power lives within EVERY believer. Sure, a pastor speaks to the church on Sunday but he will never sit in your math class or talk with most of your friends.

Only you can do that.

We start with those closest to us. If anyone has ever had Torchy's queso in Austin, you know how quickly you can become an instant representative! You have tasted and seen the goodness and want to share it with all those around you. Believe it or not, the good news of Jesus is even better!

After we share with our friends, the good news begins to bleed into the communities and work around us. Paul writes that whether you are eating or drinking do it for the glory of God. God doesn't want us to settle for normal in our studies, our relationships, or our dreams. He wants us to live so fully that we are able to look at people in our hallways with different eyes and we are able to invite hope into the hardest of situations (just like Jesus did).

This hope is meant to be experienced and shared. It's was never meant to be stuffed away in a church, but rather it was meant to fill our schools, homes, and jobs. So let's continue the mission we were given, with the gifts and talents we were provided into the place God's Spirit beckons us to go.

CHAPTER 29

SEVEN HABITS OF BRINGING YOUR UNIQUE PURPOSE TO LIFE

I'm sure there are people you look up to and think "How did they get there?" Success has many pathways and it is always interesting to learn how people became the best at what they do. Wise people will learn from others that have gone before them.

I remember thinking in 6th grade that one day, I might write a book. Never thought it would take this long to actually do it but I'm thankful God has given me the ability to put my experiences down on paper and tell a story through them that can help others. To be successful at whatever you set out to do you must be consistent doing the right things for a long enough period of time.

In analyzing my own habits, I have found seven things that I feel have helped me go from a dead end career in sales that I hated to running my own organization as a speaker and author. You may find other healthy habits that will turn out to be vital for your success but at minimum, this list will get you focused in the right direction.

JOE ELLIOTT

1. I start my day by choosing to thank God for it. Our attitude shapes our actions, and I cannot afford to lose perspective on how short life is and why I am really here. Neither can you. A twenty second prayer in the morning can be all that is needed to help you posture your mind and heart with gratitude because you have been given another day to be God's representative here on Earth. Don't abuse it.

2. I ask God for help in expecting the unexpected each day and responding appropriately. Has anyone ever had a day when everything went perfectly according to plan? I haven't. So, it makes sense to be prepared for adversity and new opportunity.

3. I focus on the one thing I need to accomplish today - and I give it the majority of my energy. Planning comes naturally to some and is kryptonite to others. Don't get so lost in the details that you forget to do what is most important. This is an exercise in learning how to prioritize and then execute based on that plan.

4. I remind myself to enjoy the ride. There are thousands of things buzzing around us daily that can suck the joy out of life. Even when things are really, really bad, I know that there is value in failure and pain. This empowers me to take risks, speak boldly, give whatever I have in me to give that day and just enjoy the rollercoaster of life.

5. I do my best to encourage and thank those around me. I admit that this is a muscle group I am still developing. The environment of people we choose to surround ourselves with influences who we are and what we become. It's hard to find relationships with others that bring out the best in you. When you do find them, nourish those relationships with all you've got. Remember, nobody ever accomplishes anything great alone. Make a habit of investing in others and you will reap the fruit of your labor when you need it the most.

6. **I realize I can never be all things to all people.** When who I am and what I do is not a good fit for someone in need, I acknowledge it and move on. The truth is that I am not the best person for the job most of the time. Neither are you. When people want you to become something you are not, you have to recognize your limits and be ok with saying no. The more self-aware you become - and you have grown leaps and bounds by just completing this book - the more you will learn to position yourself in situations that will help maximize the things you do best and not overextending yourself in areas that you are weak in.

7. **I end the day by choosing to thank God again.** I already battle with pride as is. I don't need to go to bed every night with a Superman complex. When our pride starts to swell, our humility retreats. Humility is the glue that keeps us moving forward despite our circumstances. End your day by thanking God and you will find yourself putting things in their proper perspective and keeping that ego in check.

Action: I'm not gonna lie, you have your work cut out for you. God has entrusted you with much and you may in fact be the generation that helps our nation experience Jesus once again. I can tell you that it won't be through sermons and books but the power of one young Christian willing to lay down their life, their desires for the sake of serving their peers.

Think about a few healthy habits that might be key to your short term and long term success, then write them down on the next page.

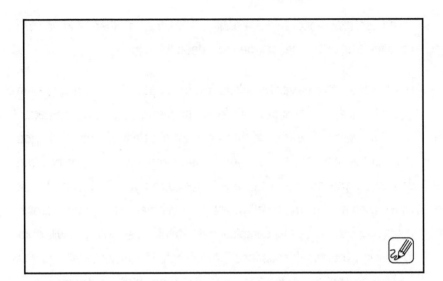

CHAPTER 30

ENJOYING THE RIDE

W e have more than likely not met in person but we do mean this with deep sincerity: we are so proud of you! You don't realize how few people complete something like this, but it's true. You are among a minority of people with the ambition needed to be someone special.

At this point, you don't even have to achieve a single goal you set and you will still impact people around you, because you have the courage to travel down a path that others only talk about. You are taking risks and you will fail your way forward. Most will exert their energy trying to avoid failure only to find that in their conservative approach, they still fail.

It pays to take risks!

Your level of confidence and doubt may see-saw but your daily choice to keep learning and moving forward will be the foundation of your success. If you want to perfect your purpose, there is one thing left to do - enjoy the ride.

Joy is something we can choose to experience when we give thanks to God for this life. The wealthiest, most famous individuals to walk this Earth have never been able to find lasting contentment in fame or fortune. That is never going to change.

If what you are setting out to do is primarily self-serving, you are in for major disappointment. However, if you desire to take the things you have been blessed with and offer them back to God for the good of those around you, you cannot fail.

In the words of one of the richest, wisest kings ever known:

I perceived that there is nothing better for them than to be joyful and to do good as long as they live; also, that everyone should eat and drink and take pleasure in all his toil—this is God's gift to man.
Ecclesiastes 3:12-13

Since we are not God and lack the ability to control all our circumstances, it makes sense to develop the things we can control and learn to enjoy the ride along the way with everything else.

We only have one opportunity to fight against evil because once the war is over, it's over. There will be no lost people to reach in heaven, so your time to shine is now. We must make the decision every morning to enjoy the unpredictability of life. It would be futile to fight against it.

So, like you, I will move on from this book and continue my own attack against living a normal life. Not everything will work out as I hope and that's ok. One thing I know for sure, I will never regret trying and neither will you.

Some days will fill you with inspiration while others will overwhelm you with despair. It's a crazy ride but God has already given you exactly what you need to take the next step.

We would seriously love to hear from you. Consider reaching out to us in a few months to tell us how it's going. We are here for you and are willing to help anyway we can.

Thank you for being you and for taking the time to bring your unique purpose to life!

SPIRITUAL GIFTS EXPLAINED

One important note on this topic. The Holy Spirit lives within you as a believer and the Holy Spirit has ALL of these gifts listed here. As we read in Paul's letter to the Corinthians, it's the Holy Spirit that decides who gets what gifts and <u>when</u>. This means that at any given point in time, we can access any or all of these gifts as God chooses. So just because the gift of intercession didn't rank high on your list doesn't mean you don't pray. If evangelism is not part of your core gifts at the moment, it doesn't mean you don't share the Gospel. Get in the habit of asking God to give you what you need to reflect His nature and character in any given situation. Lean on your top three gifts the most, but don't dismiss the others that the Holy Spirit can bring to the surface within you as He chooses.

Oh, and depending on what spiritual gifts test you decided to take, some of these gifts listed here may or may not have been on it.

Administration

The gift of administration is the ability to organize multiple people and tasks to get things done. Every great movement and leader in history has had people with this gift by their side. It doesn't come with lots of props and glory but nothing gets done without this skill in place. If you have this gift, find a group, team, project, or cause to get behind and you will shine.

Luke 14:28-30; Acts 6:1-7; 1 Corinthians 12:28

Apostleship

The gift of apostleship, like the Apostle Paul had, is the rare gift to be able to pioneer new churches, missions and ministries through planting, overseeing, and training. You have a passion to see God's Church expand here on Earth and will be willing to sacrifice what is necessary to reach others. With this gift you should consider starting or serving in a Christian club on your campus, interning for your church over the summer, saving up for missions trips and exercising your teaching skills in any way you can.

Acts 15:22-35; 1 Corinthians 12:28; 2 Corinthians 12:12; Galatians 2:7-10; Ephesians 4:11-14

Craftsmanship

The gift of craftsmanship is the ability to plan, build, and create with your hands. Fixing things and understanding how things work comes more naturally to you. You are curious about how things are put together and love to be part of the process of bringing an idea to life with your hands. God is the master builder and your gift is a reflection of His desire to create beings that could themselves, be capable of creativity. Explore all kinds of trades that require hands on work. Trust me, everyone who sucks at crafting/fixing/planning stuff is so grateful to have people like you in their life.

Exodus 30:22, 31:3-11; 2 Chronicles 34:9-13; Acts 18:2-3

Discernment

The gift of discernment is one that allows others to distinguish between right and wrong motives and the spiritual forces at work in any given situation. Normally this gift rises to the surface as you get older but at your age, it could feel like a 'gut instinct'. You can often see quickly beyond the surface or front someone puts up even if you have just met them. People with discernment make for very wise counselors and advisors. Consider mentoring or tutoring someone younger than you at church or school. God is giving you insight into people and situations, so maximize this gift by building relationships with people you want to reach and by speaking your mind a little more often. In other words, learn to trust your gut.

Matthew 16:21-23; Acts 5:1-11, 16:16-18; 1 Corinthians 12:10; 1 John 4:1-6

Evangelism

The gift of evangelism is present in those who have an above average desire and ability to communicate the Gospel to those who are not Christians. This is more than just wanting to see people saved, every Christian feels that to some extent. This gift is one that is always brewing in you. You intentionally look for ways to talk about Jesus with others and think about how the best way to communicate with them might be. On top of this, you are bold enough to do it and risk looking like a fool or being made fun of. Your courage will inspire many Christians the more you exercise this gift. Develop it by learning how to talk about biblical truths using analogies that connect with the life experiences and interests of the individuals you are speaking to. Be creative in how and when you share. Paul was a brilliant evangelist because he shifted the way he communicated based on the culture or person he was speaking to, making it easier for others to connect to the Gospel. Jesus did the same.

Acts 8:5-6, 8:26-40, 14:21, 21:8; Ephesians 4:11-14

Exhortation

The gift of exhortation is the gift of comfort, counsel and encouragement that motivates others to action through written or spoken word. This was probably in Paul's top five if you ask me. His letters to the churches and to individuals like Timothy are passionate and strong in language that comforts, counsels, and encourages. President Roosevelt's famous quote "Nobody cares how much you know until they know how much you care" rings true here. This gift can be a catalyst in the lives of those around you. You probably remember some nice things a teacher, coach, or friend ever said to you, right? Words are powerful and the gift of being able to use words to build up and guide others is a gift that can leave a legacy. Look for opportunities to get to know people and exhort them. Great counselors and comforters are also great listeners. Learn to do that well.

Acts 14:22; Romans 12:8; 1 Timothy 4:13;
Hebrews 10:24-25

Faith

The gift of faith is the ability to believe in God for supernatural results in every area of life. This is kind of cliché but I like the term "unshakeable" here. That's what this gift is at its core. No matter how difficult or crazy things get in life, people with this gift can center on the truth in Scripture and have a confidence in God that all things are possible. This can also be described as a strong conviction in your beliefs. The power behind this gift is that it fuels your actions that people see on a daily basis. The gift of faith ran strong in just about every hero in the Old and New Testament. David didn't face Goliath without faith, nor Daniel the pit of lions, nor Jesus the crucifixion. Exercise this gift on your campus by letting your confidence in God shine during times of uncertainty. Pray with and for your classmates when the needs arise. When you feel the Holy Spirit nudge you to take action on something, practice not hesitating and just do it. This will enhance your gift of faith even more.

Acts 11:22-24; Romans 4:18-21; 1 Corinthians 12:9;
Hebrews 11

Giving

The gift of giving involves being able to give whatever you have, in the form of time, money, talents, or possessions, generously to others with no strings attached. You would literally give someone the shirt off your back if they needed it more than you did. This gift is such a beautiful picture of God's love for the entire world. Be on the lookout for what those around you need. There are peers around you who are lonely and need someone to take an interest in their life, give them your time. There are those that are struggling in school or sports, give them your talents. Others may not have the financial resources you have, find a way to generate income and share it liberally. The act of giving is the Gospel in action. The people around you will always remember what you do over what you say and it will open many doors for conversations about Jesus.

Mark 12:41-44; Romans 12:8; 2 Corinthians 8:1-7, 9:2-7 65

Healing/Miracles

The gift of healing means to act as an intermediary in faith, prayer, and by the laying-on of hands for the healing of physical, mental, and spiritual sickness. Contrary to some beliefs, this gift, like the gift of Tongues, is still alive today; however, it is not as common as others. People are miraculously healed through prayer daily around the world. One of the reasons this gift is dormant in many young believers is that it's rarely exercised. We also have a preconceived idea on what a 'healing' should look like. We expect the blind to see, the disease to immediately vanish or some other instant result. That does happen, but it's not the only way God brings healing. The best way to exercise this gift is to be bold enough to look for situations around you that need healing either physically, emotionally, or spiritually and be bold enough to pray. If someone is too weirded out by you praying publicly, no worries, there is no specific formula to this, just pray! When God does use you to bring healing into someone's life, WOW, it's a game changer for them and everyone they will tell for years to come.

Acts 3:1-10, 9:32-35, 28:7-10; 1 Corinthians 12:9, 28

Helps/Service

The gift of helping and service are so close in nature that for the sake of ease, I am lumping them together. This is a gift to work in a supportive role to accomplish tasks with the ability to often see the need before others do. It's similar to the gift of administration but the difference is that this gift is a little more versatile and isn't necessarily related to managing projects or groups like administration is. With this gift you find yourself getting your hands dirty on the front lines doing the things nobody else wants to do. You can also be behind the scenes helping others get things done. You do whatever is needed, wherever and whenever it is needed. This gift makes you a blessing to others because you are so darn reliable. Everyone needs friends they can count on and YOU are that friend! Use this flexibility and willingness to serve that you have been given to bless people you want to reach. Youth pastors, teachers, coaches, parents, etc., work hard doing what they do and when people your age come along offering their time and talents, it's a HUGE blessing. Those around you will see Jesus' character clearly through your generosity in this area.

Mark 15:40-41; Acts 9:36; Romans 16:1-2;
1 Corinthians 12:28 Acts 6:1-7; Romans 12:7;
Galatians 6:10; 1 Timothy 1:16-18; Titus 3:14

Hospitality

The gift of hospitality is the ability to create warm, welcoming environments for others no matter where you are. You know how weird it can be to walk into a new environment and not know anyone. We have all been there. Those with the gift of hospitality are aware of that tension and do an amazing job making people feel not just at home, but like family. This is an awesome gift for you to use on campus, at church, or even in your neighborhood. New students and visitors give you the opportunity to shine as you greet them, introduce them to others and help them feel as though they have been here all along.

Acts 16:14-15; Romans 12:13, 16:23;
Hebrews 13:1-2; 1 Peter 4:9

Intercession

The gift of intercession is one that stands in the gap in prayer for someone, something, or someplace, believing what you ask for will come to
be. Chances are that if you scored high on this gift it's because you
come from a church background that priorities prayer in some way.
The prayer movement is rapidly growing across the U.S. and is becoming the engine for so many innovative and brilliant ministries. This very
book you are reading is the product of intercessors like you who prayed
for this to be years and years ago! Like any other gift, an intercessor will
learn to flex this muscle more and more by actually praying. Be on the
lookout for other Christians at your school who may attend a different
church yet might also have this gift. You will know because when you
ask them if they would be interested in getting together and praying for
a few minutes before school they perk up and say "Yes!" One of the
greatest campus revival movements in America started by a few guys
getting together to pray. You can buy the book and read about the story
of what happened and is happening at the University of Texas in Austin:
https://www.campusrenewal.org/resources/

Hebrews 7:25; Colossians 1:9-12, 4:12-13; James 5:14-16

Knowledge

The gift of knowledge is the hunger to soak in information, analyze facts,
and become a subject matter expert on any particular topic related to
the Bible or even outside of it. You are like a sponge. You can absorb
and retain things better than most, which makes you a living vault of info
on anything you decide to learn about. Some people with this gift will
focus on a few areas that they are really passionate about and dedicate
themselves to becoming experts in that field, while others will choose
to not go as deep, spending their time absorbing a variety of different
subjects. Either way you go, don't let this knowledge go to your head

and become prideful. Recognize that this ability came from God and use it to help teach, lead, and mentor others who desire the knowledge you have. Start with what you already know and are passionate about whether it be a hobby, video game, sport...whatever, share your knowledge freely, with humility, in a manner that seeks to build others up and you will be exuding the DNA of Jesus!

Acts 5:1-11; 1 Corinthians 12:8; Colossians 2:2-3

Leadership

The gift of leadership is just like it sounds, the ability to influence people and direct them toward a common goal or vision. This gift takes guts. Those who choose to exercise this gift will find it to be a tough path at times, even lonely. But take heart, you are wired for this! Leaders are often critiqued by everyone around them who thinks they can do a better job, and maybe they could at times, but THEY didn't step up when leadership was needed, YOU did. A great leader will learn how to work with a variety of different personality types and giftings around them. You can bring out the best in people when you want to and help create unity among a diverse group. You start out using this gift to lead small, team assignments at school or helping your friends all come to agreement when everyone is being divisive. It continues to grow as you step up to serve your coaches, teachers, etc., and find that others are following your lead. You don't have to be the first to step up in EVERY situation but you do need to be ready to respond fast when you are needed. Begin by looking for opportunities to lead others by your example in sports, clubs, or anything you are involved in. It's your actions and care for others as a leader that will win people over.

Romans 12:8; 1 Timothy 3:1-13, 5:17; Hebrews 13:17

Mercy

The gift of mercy is the ability to feel empathy or to care for those who are hurting in some way. People with this gift are surprised to find it's a gift because having mercy comes so naturally to them that they think everyone has it. They don't. As Christians, we should all be merciful but that doesn't mean that we are all good at it. Your gift is one that brings forgiveness, love, patience, and kindness to even the most difficult people or situations. It's true that people with this gift can often get taken advantage of but you are willing to take that risk where others are not. That's one reason why it's a gift from God. Look around you for 'hopeless' causes, people that others have written off, and be intentional about drawing closer to them. When Jesus spent time with the lame, crippled, criminals, and people the culture did not think highly of, He sent a message to the world about who God is and what He cares about. You can do the same and it begins with the people you see on a daily basis.

Matthew 9:35-36; Mark 9:41; Romans 12:8; 1 Thess. 5:14

Pastor/Shepherd

The gift of pastor/shepherd is the ability to care for the personal needs of others by nurturing and mending life issues. Just because you have this gift doesn't mean you should be a pastor of a church. The truth is that many pastors today have more of a teaching gift than they do a pastoral one. You have this gift because you are ready and willing to live life in the trenches with others. You are not interested in talking to them about Jesus and moving on, you want to dig in deep and really help people around you succeed. You often find yourself looking out for their best interests more than you do your own! Use this gift by investing more time in a smaller group of people. You are not trying to win a popularity contest here, you are willing to do what few are in that you want to be there for people even when they are not there for you. You can handle the rejection when it comes, but you still bounce back and show others that you are here to stay and are ready to help them grow personally, professionally, and/or spiritually whenever they are ready.

John 10:1-18; Ephesians 4:11-14;
1 Timothy 3:1-7; 1 Peter 5:1-3

Prophecy

The gift of prophecy is the gift to communicate God's truth and heart in a way that realigns others back to God. I know you might have been hoping this had something to do with predicting the future but it really doesn't. God could tell you what is about to happen before it happens and ask you to share that but most commonly, this gift is about being God's vocal messenger. A person with a prophetic gift is really, really bothered by sin and has a burning desire to call it out, along with injustice, when they come across it. It takes courage to have this gift because you are often saying the hard things that everybody needs to hear but that nobody wants to hear. It's not always bad news though. God may be leading you to encourage others through His words or your actions. You really are a messenger. As you grow in your knowledge of the Bible and consistency in your prayer life, this gift will rise more and more to the surface. Be careful not to be too quick with your tongue as even the truth can sometimes be delivered in a manner that is outside of God's character. On campus, be the person who is standing up against injustice wherever it is and learn to deliver the hard truth gently and compassionately to others when the time calls for it.

Acts 2:37-40, 7:51-53, 26:24-29;
1 Corinthians 14:1-4; 1 Thessalonians 1:5

Teaching

The gift of teaching is the ability to study, learn, and then share knowledge with others in a way they can understand and apply. The church would never grow without this gift present. Everyone has some degree of knowledge on any given subject but not many can find a way to articulate what they know to others. With this gift you can educate a variety of different people and cultures because you can adapt well to different learning styles. You enjoy helping someone understand a hard concept and are patient enough to hang with them until they do. While in school, consider tutoring others your age or younger. Assist your teachers if possible. Lead a Bible study at church or on campus. Put yourself in a position to teach something to someone in a creative way and you will grow in this gifting as you do.

Acts 18:24-28, 20:20-21; 1 Corinthians 12:28;
Ephesians 4:11-14

Tongues (and Interpretation)

Depending on the denomination you come from, there are some varying opinions on how this gift functions. The gift of tongues is the ability to pray in a heavenly language, or different language that is foreign to you, and is often accompanied by someone who can interpret. It is closely linked to the gift of intercession and sometimes prophecy so I would go back and read what we had to say about those. This is most definitely a gift that can display God's mighty power and awe to those both in and outside of the church.

Acts 2:1-13; 1 Corinthians 12:10, 14:1-14

Wisdom

The gift of wisdom differs from the gift of knowledge. This is the ability to take knowledge and put it into use for yourself and others. It provides people a clear path to walk down and is layered in wise counsel. You have this because you can take in a ton of information regarding a problem or situation and after assessing, can offer solutions that are backed by Scripture and experience. Proverbs personifies the gift of wisdom and it is a great resource to lean on. You develop this gift by studying Scripture or other subject matters and applying what you learn. Use this gift like a counselor would, take time to get to know the people around you, be a great listening ear, research their issues if you are not familiar with them and be ready to share what you learn. As your experiences broaden in life, so will this gift.

Acts 6:3,10; 1 Corinthians 2:6-13, 12:8

APPENDIX B

HOW TO USE THIS BOOK AS A SIX WEEK DEVOTIONAL

If you are a leader looking to walk students through this book, our recommendation is to present it as a six week series with each section being the focus of a week. You could also treat each chapter as a day and make it a thirty day challenge but assuming you have more time to work with, here is how we would lay it out:

Week 1 - Complete Section One, Chapters 1-5.

Week 2 - Complete Section Two, Chapters 6-10.

Week 3 - Complete Section Three, Chapters 11-14.

Week 4 - Complete Section Four, Chapters 15-20.

Week 5 - Complete Section Five, Chapters 21-25.

Week 6 - Complete Section Six, Chapters 26-30.

The action items at the end of most chapters make for great large group or small group discussions. The more time you give students to share and bounce their own self reflections off of others, the more they will learn about themselves and how God has uniquely made them.

If you have any questions or thoughts about how to use this book with your group, just reach out. We will make it a priority to get back to you within 24 hours.

WE WANT TO HEAR FROM YOU!

Seriously, we'd love to connect with you and look forward to hearing how this book is helping you to find your true calling. If you have questions about different parts of this book, or if you found a typo, or if you just need to talk with someone, please connect with us!

- ✓ Facebook: http://www.facebook.com/catalystcollectiveatx
- ✓ YouTube: http://www.youtube.com/catalystcollective
- ✓ Tumblr: http://catalystcollectiveblog.tumblr.com/
- ✓ Linkedin: http://www.linkedin.com/in/joe-elliott-9753048
- ✓ Instagram: https://www.instagram.com/catalystcollectiveatx
- ✓ Snapchat: https://www.snapchat.com/add/CatalystATX
- ✓ Website: http://www.catalyscollective.community/
- ✓ My Website: http://www.joeelliottlive.com/
- ✓ Email: joe@catalystteencenter.com

CPSIA information can be obtained
at www.ICGtesting.com
Printed in the USA
LVHW050838061118
595976LV00008B/519

9 781941 512272